W9-CFB-789

Lisa's Story

The Kent State University Press
Kent, Ohio

lisa's story
the other shoe

by *Tom Batiuk*

© 2007 by Batom, Inc.

ALL RIGHTS RESERVED

Library of Congress Catalog Card Number 2007001380

ISBN: 978-0-87338-952-5 (pbk)

ISBN: 978-0-87338-924-2 (cloth)

Manufactured in China

11 10 09 08 07   5 4 3 2 1

LIBRARY OF CONGRESS CATALOGING-IN-PUBLICATION DATA

Batiuk, Tom.
Lisa's story : the other shoe / Tom Batiuk.
   p.   cm. — (Literature and medicine)
ISBN-13: 978-0-87338-924-2 (alk. paper) ∞
ISBN-13: 978-0-87338-952-5 (pbk.: alk. paper) ∞
1. Breast—Cancer—Comic books, strips, etc.   I. Title.
rc280.b8b375 2007
616.99'449—dc22   2007001380

British Library Cataloging-in-Publication data are available.

Contents

For Cathy
The rose of my heart

Preface

When I was asked about the origins of the first *Lisa's Story,* I said that, at a certain stage in life, things like cancer would happen to our friends and relatives and that those experiences become a part of our emotional inner landscape.

Later, when I myself was diagnosed with cancer, the news was more like a kick in the gut. It was then that I began to fully appreciate the fundamental void that separates empathy and personal experience.

In deciding to give voice to that experience, I was led back to Lisa. In point of fact, it was Lisa—just as she had the first time—who provided a way for me to explore these new thoughts, to release these new emotions. My passing observation of a plaque to a departed loved one on a bench in Central Park opened the door and allowed me to find my way in.

This time I found that things came from deeper within. This new work was stronger, richer, more resonant and hard-won. It was also work that was totally in-your-face and uncomfortable and that couldn't be dismissed. This time Lisa's story was going to be as honest as I could make it.

What follows is her story.

Acknowledgments

I'd like to thank Chuck Ayers, Alex Sinclair, Brian Haberlin, Rob Ro, Lee Loughridge, Dave Stewart, John Byrne, Sean Mckeever, Bill and Paula Sandor, and Ashley Wesemeyer for their beautiful, fun, and amazing contributions to this work and for making my painful slowness less painful.

Thanks as well to Rocky Shepard, Claudia Smith, and George Haeberlein at King Features for making a stand with me at the intersection of art and commerce and for helping me take my work to the street.

I also want to thank Will Underwood, Joanna Hildebrand Craig, Christine Brooks, and Susan Cash at the Kent State University Press for their belief in the work even when no work existed to believe in.

Thanks to Martin Kohn and Carol Donley for researching the resources in the addendum so that those who pass through cancer's shadow might find the help they need.

Thanks to my wife, Cathy, for inspiring me to make Lisa strong.

A long overdue thanks to Dick Sherry, who let me in the door way back when.

In memory of Rebecca Marec, whose friendship, generosity of spirit, and courage are so much a part of this story, and Jay Kennedy, whose guidance and belief in and support of this story helped shepherd it onto the comics page.

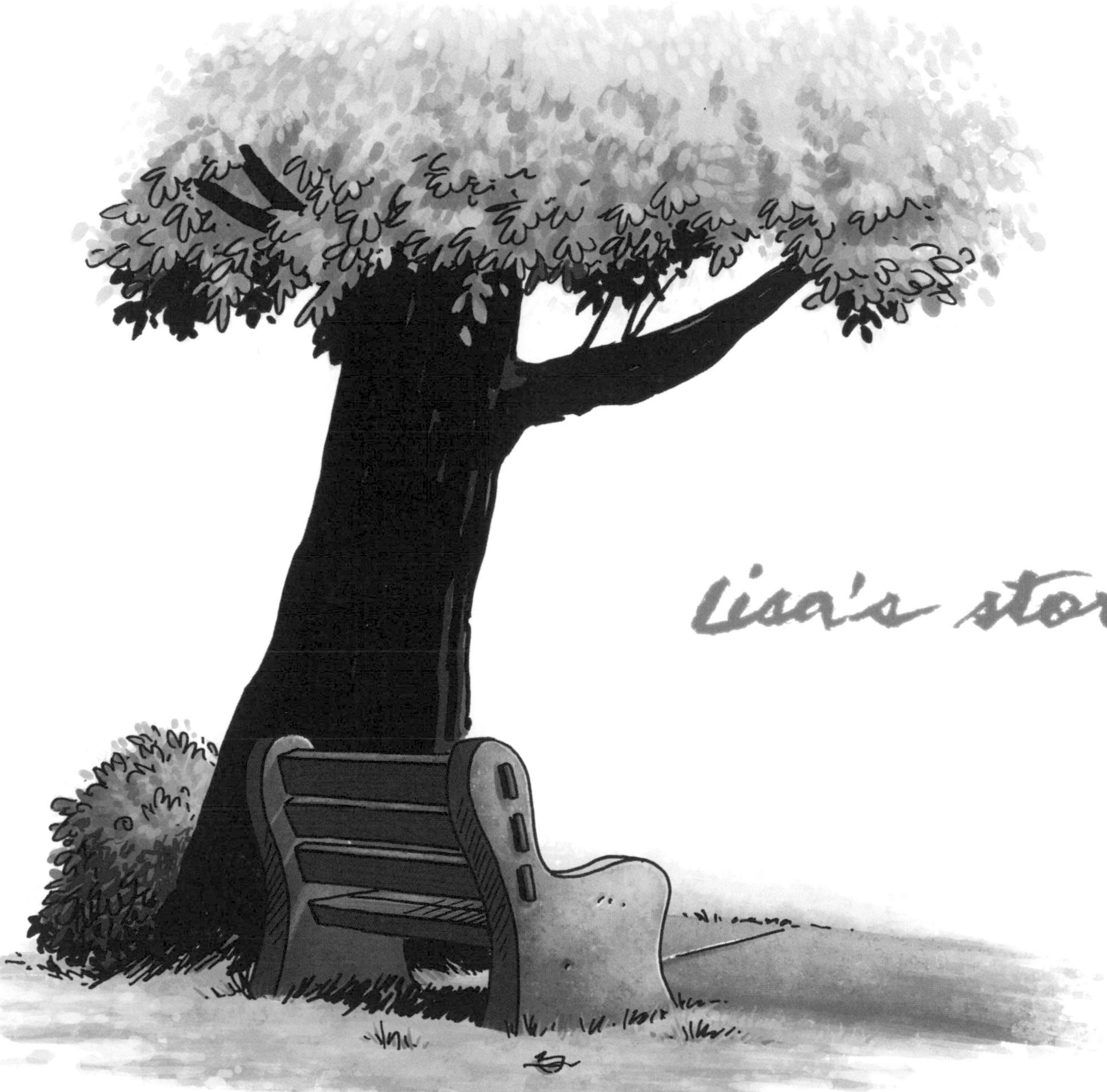

Lisa's story

THIS IS THE PERFECT WAY TO GET IN SHAPE FOR SUPER SUNDAY!
SO YOU'RE REALLY LOOKING FORWARD TO THE SUPER BOWL, FUNKY?
WEST
TOW
1-18
NO, LI ... I'M REALLY LOOKING FORWARD TO ALL OF THE PIZZAS WE'RE GOING TO SELL ON SUPER BOWL SUNDAY!
BATIUK

OOF!!
BATIUK
WHAT A CATCH! WHERE'S 'WIDE WORLD OF SPORTS' WHEN YOU NEED 'EM?
ARE YOU OKAY, LISA?
UH-HUH ... I MUST'VE JUST LANDED ON A SMALL ROCK OR SOMETHING!
1-19

JUST BECAUSE THE GAME IS OVER DOESN'T MEAN WE HAVE TO STOP PLAYING...
I COULD STILL THROW A FEW PASSES YOUR WAY...
AS LONG AS YOU PROMISE THERE'LL BE PLENTY OF HOLDING PENALTIES...
1-20

ARE YOU SURE YOU'RE OKAY?
I'M FINE... I THINK I WAS JUST A LITTLE SORE FROM THE FOOTBALL GAME!
MONTONI'S Pizza
CARE TO HIT THE TEAM SHOWERS?
THANKS... BUT I THINK I'M GOING TO NAP A BIT!
1-21

I LEFT SOME HOT WATER FOR YOU, KID!
THANKS!
BATIUK
1-22

BATIUK
BREAST SELF-EXAMINATION (BSE)
1-23

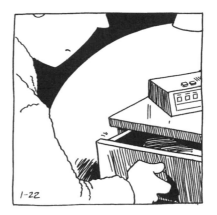

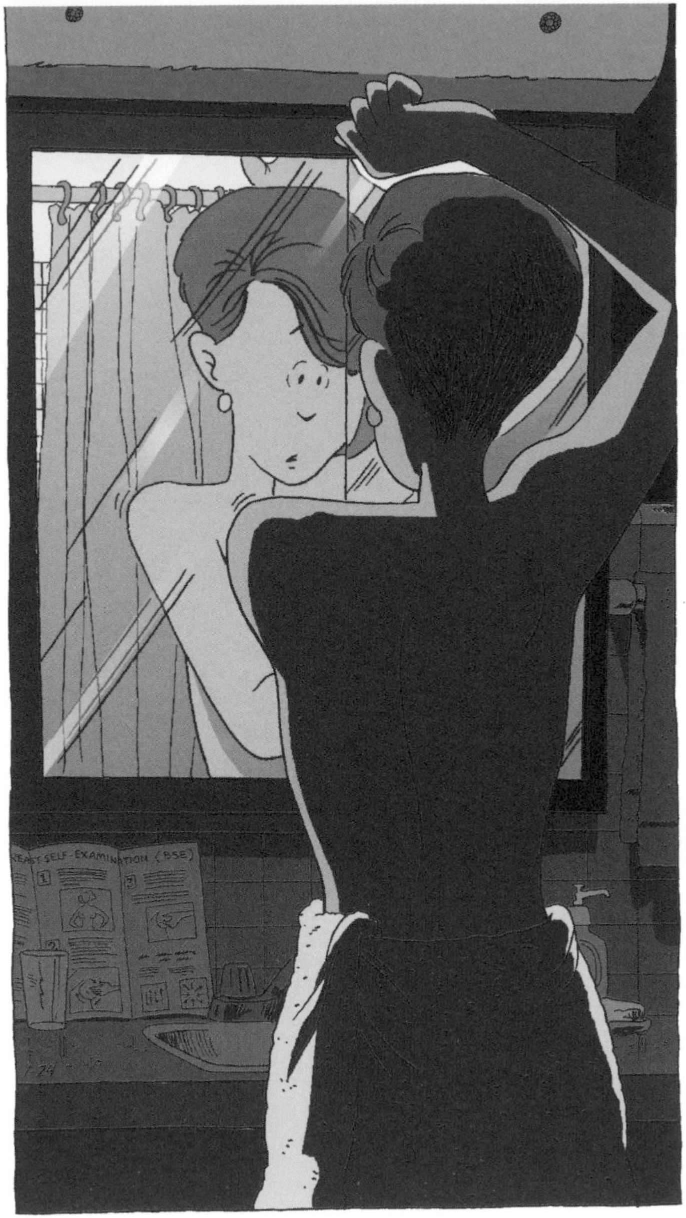
EAST SELF-EXAMINATION (BSE)

HAVE A GOOD DAY!
YEAH, YOU TOO, KID!
BATIUK
I'D LIKE TO SEE THE DOCTOR AS SOON AS I CAN!
1-25

LEESE ... I'M HOME!
LISA?
BATIUK
26
Appt.
Dr. Parks
3:30
1-26

SO LISA WENT TO SEE A DOCTOR WITHOUT TELLING YOU? SAY, YOU DON'T SUPPOSE SHE'S...
WELL, WE WEREN'T PLANNING ON IT, BUT YOU NEVER KNOW...
'WHY ELSE WOULD SHE DO THAT?'
IT FEELS LIKE A CYST... A LOT OF WOMEN HAVE THEM... WE'LL SEND YOU FOR SOME MAMMOGRAMS!
MEDICAL BUIL
C. PARKS MD
L. SMITH MD
J. JOHNSON MD
1-27

I'M LISA MOORE... DR. PARKS SCHEDULED A MAMMOGRAM FOR ME!
FINE... JUST HAVE A SEAT AND WE'LL CALL YOU WHEN WE'RE READY!
1-28
DON'T PANIC... JUST RELAX! READ A MAGAZINE AND GET YOUR MIND ON SOMETHING ELSE!
People
Sports Illustrated
FITNESS

MRS. MOORE ?
IS IT OKAY FOR ME TO GO NOW ?
NOT JUST YET...
BATIUK
1-29
WE'D LIKE TO TAKE A FEW MORE X-RAYS !
B

HI. I SAW THAT YOU WENT TO THE DOCTOR... WHAT'S UP ?
I'VE GOT A LUMP IN MY BREAST !
1-30

FUNKY WINKERBEAN BY TOM BATIUK

THANKS FOR TAKING A WALK WITH ME, LES!

I JUST COULDN'T FACE ALL OF THE BUSTLE AND GOOD CHEER AT MONTONI'S RIGHT NOW!

JUST BECAUSE THEY SPOTTED SOMETHING ON YOUR MAMMOGRAM DOESN'T NECESSARILY MEAN THAT IT'S SOMETHING BAD...

IN FACT, DR. PARKS, HIMSELF SAID THAT MOST OF THESE THINGS ARE BENIGN!

AND EVEN IF IT'S NOT... WE'VE LIVED THROUGH STUFF LIKE THIS BEFORE, AND WE CAN DO IT AGAIN!

YOU SURE KNOW HOW TO SAY THE RIGHT THING AT THE RIGHT TIME... YOU'VE CONVINCED ME!

NOW I WISH I COULD CONVINCE MYSELF!

1-31

One week later

HOW DO WE KNOW THAT THIS SURGEON WE'RE GOING TO SEE IS A GOOD ONE?

I'M SURE HE IS... BESIDES, DIDN'T DR. PARKS SAY THAT DR. RAL IS THE SURGEON HE'D WANT <u>HIS</u> WIFE TO SEE?

2-1

MAYBE WE SHOULD'VE ASKED HOW HE AND HIS WIFE WERE GETTING ALONG!

BASED ON YOUR X-RAYS, MRS. MOORE, AND MY EXAMINATION... I'D HAVE TO CONCLUDE THAT...

SUSPICIOUS CALCIFICATION...

EIGHTY-FIVE PERCENT...

LYMPH NODES...

LUMPECTOMY...

MASTECTOMY...

REALLY CAN'T BE SURE UNTIL...

DECISION YOU'LL HAVE TO MAKE...

BIOPSY...

I NEED TO SIT DOWN!

2-2

HONEY, YOU ARE SITTING DOWN!

THEN WHY WON'T THE ROOM STOP SPINNING?

HERE ... I'VE FILLED ALL OF THE INSURANCE FORMS!
"PARDON OUR DUST"
DANGER
CONSTRUCTION AREA
2-3
NOW, YOU'RE AWARE THAT YOU'LL NEED TO CALL YOUR INSURANCE COMPANY AND GET PREAPPROVAL FOR THE BIOPSY!
YES!
I'M SURPRISED WE DON'T HAVE TO GET PREAPPROVAL BEFORE WE GET SICK!
BATIUK

I'VE GOT TO CONCENTRATE AND FOCUS ON THE THINGS I NEED TO DO...
BATIUK
2-4
NOTIFYING MY PROFS AT THE COLLEGE ... A LIST OF THINGS WE HAVE TO PICK UP... ANYTHING TO DISTRACT MYSELF FROM THINKING THE WORST!
I'VE GOT MY CANCER ALL PACKED FOR THE HOSPITAL!

THE TISSUE REMOVED FROM THE TUMOR WAS DETERMINED TO BE MALIGNANT...

2-5

WE'LL KNOW MORE AFTER WE GET THE RESULTS OF THE ESTROGEN RECEPTOR ASSAY, BUT I'M GUESSING IT'S A STAGE ONE CANCER... AND, SINCE YOU'RE YOUNG AND HEALTHY I'D SAY THAT YOUR PROGNOSIS IS EXCELLENT!

I APPRECIATE THAT... BUT, IF I WAS HEALTHY, I WOULDN'T BE HERE!

OVER THE COMING DAYS, YOUR WIFE IS GOING TO NEED ALL THE SUPPORT YOU CAN GIVE HER...

AND I'LL PRESCRIBE SOMETHING THAT WILL HELP HER RELAX!

IS THERE ANY CHANCE THAT I COULD HAVE SOME?

2-6

13

FUNKY WINKERBEAN
by TOM BATIUK
THIS ALL SEEMS LIKE A BAD DREAM!
CAN THIS REALLY BE HAPPENING TO ME?
WHEN YOU'RE DIAGNOSED WITH SOMETHING LIKE CANCER ... YOU SUDDENLY COME FACE TO FACE WITH YOUR OWN MORTALITY!
BATIUK
IT'S LIKE YOU'VE BEEN SHIFTED TO SOME COLD, DARK DIMENSION WHERE ONLY YOU EXIST!
YOU CAN STILL SEE EVERYONE IN THE OTHER DIMENSION GOING ABOUT THEIR SAME BORING ROUTINES ... BUT YOU'RE NOT A PART OF IT ANYMORE!
WHAT I WOULDN'T GIVE RIGHT NOW FOR THOSE SAME BORING ROUTINES!

HELLO... MAY I COME IN?

YES?

I DON'T KNOW IF YOU REMEMBER ME, LISA... BUT WE WENT TO HIGH SCHOOL TOGETHER!

2-8

I'M HOLLY BUDD!

I'M SORRY, HOLLY... PLEASE, SIT DOWN!

I DIDN'T MEAN TO APPEAR RUDE... I JUST DIDN'T EXPECT TO SEE YOU THERE!

ACTUALLY, I WAS WAITING FOR A 'REACH TO RECOVERY' VOLUNTEER WHO WAS SUPPOSED TO STOP BY TO SEE ME!

GOOD,...HERE I AM

2-9

15

THERE'S SO MUCH INFORMATION TO TAKE IN AND IT'S ALL SO CONFUSING!
I KNOW...
SHOULD I HAVE CHEMO OR RADIATION ... AND SHOULD I HAVE A LUMPECTOMY OR A FULL MASTECTOMY!
HOSPITAL
AND IF I GET A FULL MASTECTOMY ... WHAT WILL ...?
IT LOOK LIKE?
2-10

I'M SORRY I'M BEING SUCH A CRYBABY!
SNIFF
2-11
I FELT EXACTLY THE SAME WAY WHEN I WAS DIAGNOSED WITH BREAST CANCER... LOOK, WE GO WAY BACK AND CAN SHARE THINGS ... AS FRIENDS...
I CHOSE TO HAVE A MASTECTOMY!

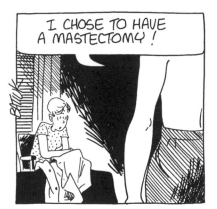

A DIAGNOSIS OF BREAST CANCER IS ONE OF THE MOST DEVASTATING THINGS A WOMAN CAN HEAR...

BUT I MADE IT THROUGH THE OPERATION AND THE CHEMO AND I'M STILL HERE TO TELL THE STORY!

HOW LONG...?

2-12

IT'S BEEN FIVE YEARS, NINE MONTHS AND TWO DAYS... BUT WHO'S COUNTING?

EVEN IF EVERYTHING I HAVE TO GO THROUGH IS SUCCESSFUL... THERE WILL ALWAYS BE THAT FEAR THAT MAYBE ONE DAY...

2-13

THAT'S SOMETHING WE ALL HAVE TO DEAL WITH IN OUR OWN WAY, LISA... BUT I'VE FOUND THAT IF YOU PUT ONE FOOT IN FRONT OF THE OTHER AND JUST KEEP GOING...

HOSPITAL

YOU CAN'T STAY AFRAID FOR THE REST OF YOUR LIFE!

[redacted]
LES + LISA
by TOM BATIUK
SALE
50%
OPEN
HISTORY
FICTION
WOMEN'S HEALTH
New
ISAAC ASIMOV
OH, I FORGOT... THERE'S ONE MORE THING I WANTED TO GET!
TO MY VALENTINE
THE BREAST CANCER GUIDE
BOOK STORE
2-14

I PICKED UP SEVERAL BOOKS ON BREAST CANCER AT THE BOOKSTORE SO WE CAN DO SOME RESEARCH AND STUDY YOUR OPTIONS !
WHY DON'T YOU JUST LIE DOWN AND TAKE IT EASY WHILE I GO OUT AND TRY TO SCARE UP SOME SUPPER !
2-15
BATIUK

WE REALLY APPRECIATE ALL OF THIS !
IF THERE'S ANYTHING ELSE THAT YOU GUYS NEED, JUST HOLLER !
I DIDN'T HAVE ANY FOOD TO BRING SO I WASHED YOUR CAR !
MONTONI'S
Pizza
PIZZA
BATIUK
2-16

MAY I HELP YOU?
YES... I CAN'T SEEM TO ACCESS THE INFORMATION I NEED ON THE INTERNET!
WESTVIEW PUBLIC LIBRARY
2-17
WHAT SUBJECT ARE YOU TRYING TO RESEARCH?
BREAST CANCER!
OH, YES... OUR BLOCKING SOFTWARE WILL KICK THAT WORD RIGHT OUT OF THERE!
BATIUK

WE HAD TO INSTALL BLOCKING SOFTWARE BECAUSE THE PEOPLE TRYING TO ACCESS THE MORE PROVOCATIVE SITES WERE CREATING A NUISANCE!
SAY NO MORE... I TEACH HIGH SCHOOL!
ACTUALLY, THE KIDS WEREN'T THE PROBLEM... IT WAS ALL OF THE CONCERNED PARENT GROUPS TRYING TO FIND SITES THAT OFFENDED THEM!
PUBLIC LIBRARY
2-18
BATIUK

Three days later

WE MOSTLY DO LUMPECTOMY AND RADIATION NOW, BUT SINCE WE DIDN'T HAVE CLEAR MARGINS AROUND THE BIOPSY... MASTECTOMY IS A BETTER CHOICE!
Dr. C. Ral
BATIUK
2-19
WE COULD SCHEDULE THE SURGERY IN TWO WEEKS!
SO SOON? BUT I HAVE SO MANY THINGS THAT I WAS PLANNING TO DO...
FINISHING TERM PAPERS... TAKING FINAL EXAMS... LIVING TO A RIPE OLD AGE...

Dr. C. Ral
BATIUK
2-20

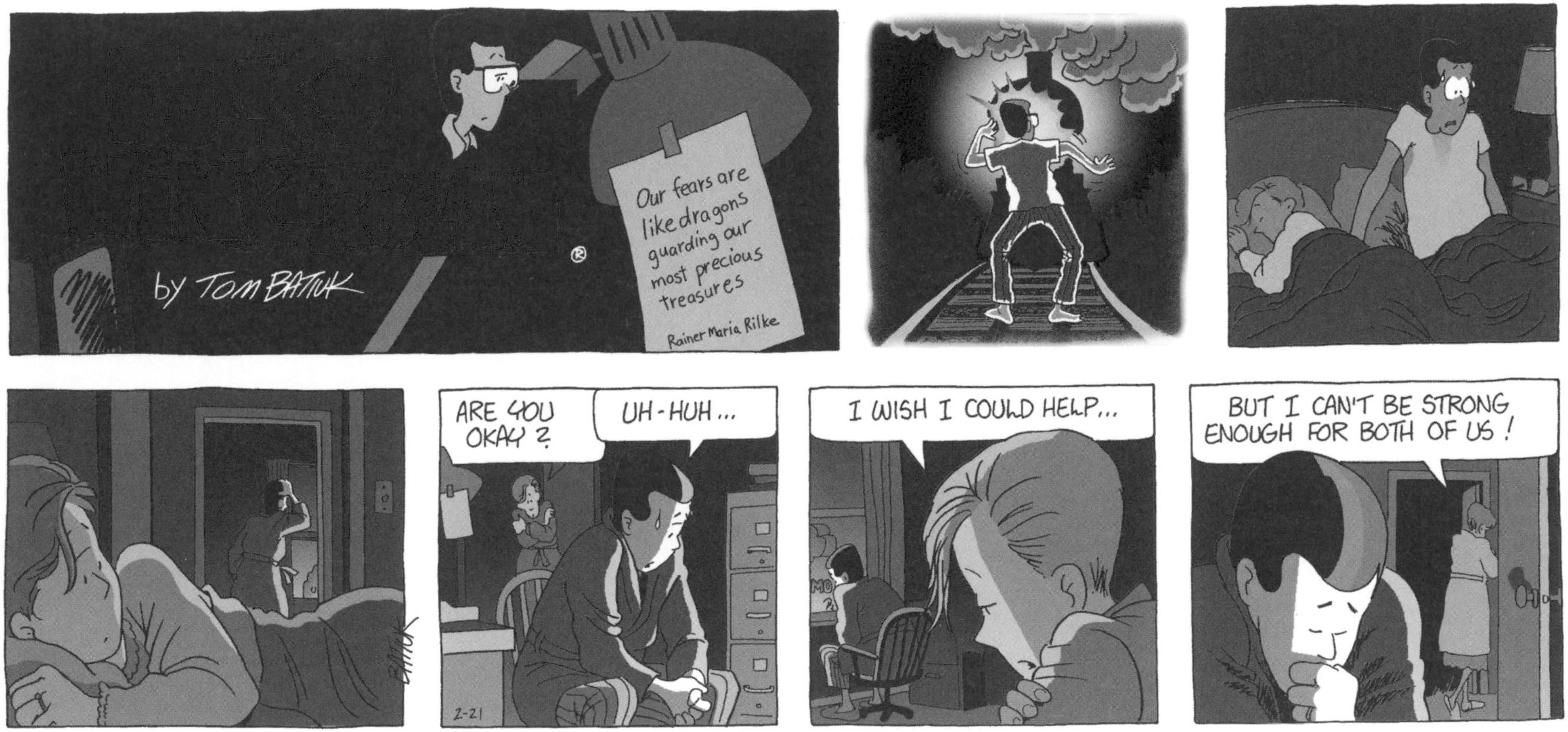
by TOM BATIUK
Our fears are like dragons guarding our most precious treasures
Rainer Maria Rilke
BATIUK
ARE YOU OKAY ?
UH-HUH...
2-21
I WISH I COULD HELP...
BUT I CAN'T BE STRONG ENOUGH FOR BOTH OF US !

I LIKE YOUR NEW HAIRCUT, BECKY!
THANKS, CINDY!
BATIUK
WHAT DO YOU THINK OF MY HAIR?
MONTONI'S Pizza
WHAT DID YOU DO, JOHN... WASH IT?
MONTONI'S Pizza
2-22

YOU KNOW, FWUNKY, ISH NOT GOOD FWOR BUSINESH TO MAKE FWUN OF YOUR CUSHTOMERS!
2-23
YOU RUN A COMIC BOOK SHOP, JOHN... WHAT WOULD YOU KNOW ABOUT TREATING CUSTOMERS!?
WHAT WOULD HE KNOW ABOUT CUSTOMERS?
BATIUK

JOHN DOES HAVE A POINT, FUNKY... MAYBE YOU SHOULDN'T PICK ON HIM ALL THE TIME!

THANK OOO VEBBY MUSH!

2-24

ANY WORD ABOUT LISA?

I GUESS SHE'S GOING TO HAVE SURGERY!

2-25

GEE, THAT'S TOUGH... I CAN'T IMAGINE HOW YOU DEAL WITH SOMETHING LIKE THAT!

ACCORDING TO LES, YOU CRY A LOT...

AND I GUESS LISA CRIES A LOT, TOO!

APPARENTLY, THEY'VE CAUGHT LISA'S CANCER EARLY ENOUGH SO THAT WITH THE RIGHT TREATMENT SHE SHOULD BE OKAY!

MAYBE I CAN DO A PIECE AT THE STATION ON HOW IMPORTANT EARLY DETECTION IS FOR WOMEN!

2-26

WHICH REMINDS ME... I SHOULD PROBABLY MAKE AN APPOINTMENT TO TAKE THE TWINS IN FOR THEIR GLAMOUR SHOT!

CHOKE

LISA SEEMS TOO YOUNG TO HAVE SOMETHING LIKE CANCER!

I KNOW... THAT ALWAYS SEEMED LIKE SOMETHING THAT HAPPENED TO SOMEONE ELSE!

IT'S KIND OF FORCING OUR MERRY LITTLE BAND TO GROW UP, ISN'T IT?

YEP... APPARENTLY EVEN ENDLESS SUMMERS EVENTUALLY END!

©1999 Batom, Inc. Distributed by North America Syndicate, Inc. All Rights Reserved.

2-27

Two weeks later

HI... ANYBODY HOME?

FUNKY WINKERBEAN
by TOM BATIUK

I JUST THOUGHT I'D COME UP TO SEE IF THERE WAS ANYTHING I COULD DO TO HELP!

NOT UNLESS YOU'VE DISCOVERED A CURE FOR CANCER!

WELL, NOW THAT YOU'VE POINTED OUT THE ELEPHANT IN THE ROOM, LISA... HOW ARE YOU FEELING?

ACTUALLY, IF I HADN'T BEEN TOLD THAT I HAVE CANCER, I'D NEVER KNOW IT... I FEEL FINE!

THERE YOU GO, LISA... THAT'S A GREAT SIGN THAT YOU'RE GOING TO BEAT THIS THING!

MONTONI'S Pizza

YOU KNOW, THEY GAVE ME SOME PILLS TO HELP CALM ME DOWN... BUT WHAT REALLY HELPS IS HAVING GOOD FRIENDS LIKE YOU, FUNKY!

FRIENDSHIP, SCHMENDSHIP... THIS IS STRICTLY BUSINESS! I'M JUST MAKING SURE THAT NOTHING HAPPENS TO MY BEST WAITRESS!

3-21

26

I'VE GOT EVERYTHING IN THE CAR!
BATIUK
WE'D BETTER GET GOING IF WE'RE GOING TO GET TO THE HOSPITAL BY SIX-THIRTY!
3-22
ARE YOU READY?
NO...

IF THEY HAD WANTED US AT THE HOSPITAL ANY EARLIER, THEY COULD'VE JUST SAVED ON THE ANESTHESIA BY LETTING ME SLEEP THROUGH THE OPERATION!
THAT'S PROBABLY WHAT OUR HMO WAS HOPING FOR!
CONSTRUCTION AREA
BATIUK
3-23
©1999 Batom, Inc. Distributed by North America Syndicate, Inc. All Rights Reserved.

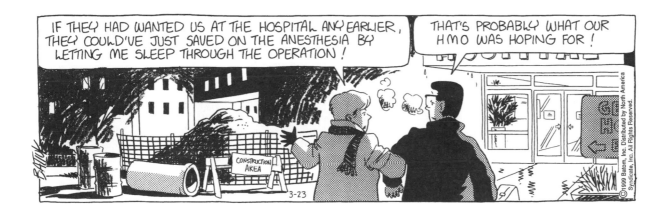

I DECIDED TO SPLURGE AND HAVE SOME PLASTIC SURGERY... I'M HAVING MY BREASTS DONE!
SURGERY CHECK IN
3-24
ARE YOU GETTING YOURS DONE TOO?
JUST ONE!
BATIUK

TOMORROW ON JERRY SPRINGER... BIGAMISTS WHO CHEAT ON BOTH OF THEIR WIVES!
WHY DO THEY HAVE THIS STUFF BLARING IN EVERY WAITING AREA?
IT'S THE DRUG COMPANIES' IDEA!
BATIUK
3-25
WE'RE BACK AND I'D LIKE TO REMIND THE AUDIENCE NOT TO THROW THINGS AT THE GUESTS!
IT HELPS SELL MORE ANTI-DEPRESSANTS!

I DON'T KNOW WHY THEY HAD US SHOW UP HERE AT THE HOSPITAL SO EARLY!
3-26
WE'VE BEEN WAITING HERE FOR OVER AN HOUR AND A HALF!
WE'RE READY FOR YOU, MRS. MOORE!
SO SOON?
← PRE OP
BATIUK

IT LOOKS LIKE YOU BENT THOSE PRETTY GOOD!
YEAH... I WAS KISSING MY WIFE GOODBYE AS THEY WHEELED HER INTO THE ELEVATOR AND THE DOORS CLOSED ON MY HEAD!
BATIUK
THERE...FIXED! NOW ALL I HAVE TO DO IS HOPE THAT THE RINGING IN MY EARS STOPS SOON!
3-27

BY TOM BATIUK
EXCUSE ME ... BUT IT SEEMS LIKE MY WIFE HAS BEEN IN THERE AN AWFULLY LONG TIME!
THE DOCTOR WILL COME OUT TO TALK WITH YOU AS SOON AS HE'S DONE!
BATIUK
SHE'S GOING TO BE **OKAY!!**
3-28

BATIUK
HI, HONEY!
GET WELL SOON
3-29

CLUNK!
3-30

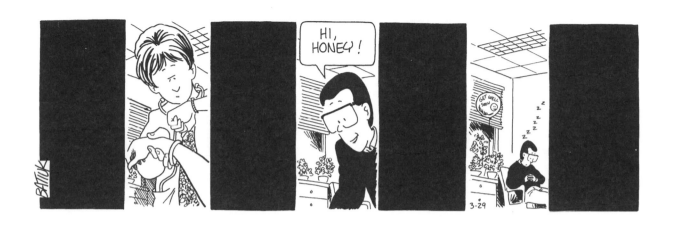

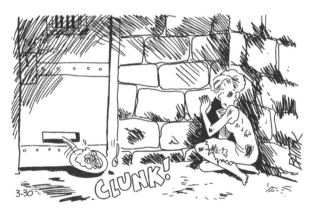

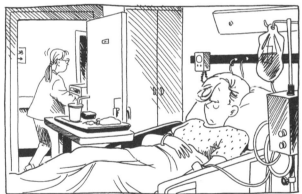

I'M AFRAID THAT THE SUNROOM ISN'T ALL THAT SUNNY TODAY!
THAT'S OKAY...
SOMETIMES IT TAKES A DIAGNOSIS LIKE CANCER TO MAKE YOU REALIZE HOW BEAUTIFUL THE RAIN CAN BE!

YOU MEAN I'M OKAY?
WE RECHECKED THE BIOPSY AND DISCOVERED THAT THERE WAS NO NEED FOR SURGERY!
I DON'T BELIEVE THIS...
APRIL FOOLS...

I'M MISERABLE, I'M DIRTY, I HURT AND I JUST WANT TO GO HOME !!
BATIUK
I WANT YOU TO TALK TO SOMEBODY AND **GET ME OUT OF HERE !!**
4-2
I'M NOT SURE SHE'S QUITE READY TO GO HOME YET !
TRUST ME... SHE'S READY !

I'M PRETTY TIRED... I THINK I'M JUST GOING TO LIE DOWN !
THAT SOUNDS LIKE A GOOD IDEA !
MONTONI'S Pizza
4-3

The next week

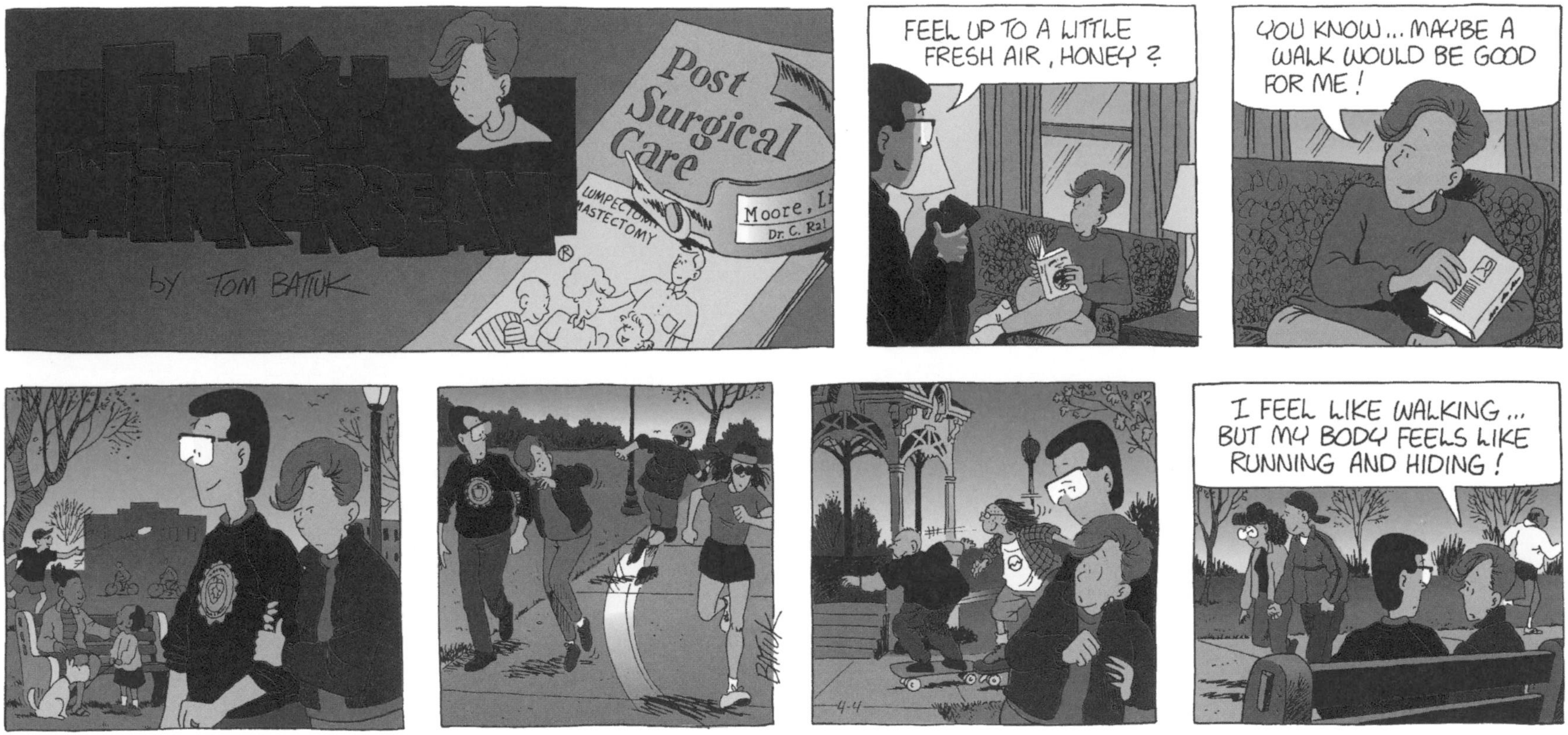
by TOM BATIUK
Post Surgical Care
MASTECTOMY
FEEL UP TO A LITTLE FRESH AIR, HONEY?
YOU KNOW... MAYBE A WALK WOULD BE GOOD FOR ME!
I FEEL LIKE WALKING... BUT MY BODY FEELS LIKE RUNNING AND HIDING!

One week after surgery

AND SO THE INVOLVEMENT OF ONLY ONE LYMPH NODE MAY MEAN THAT SOME CANCER CELLS MAY HAVE GOTTEN LOOSE ...OR IT MAY MEAN THAT YOUR IMMUNE SYSTEM HAS ALREADY DEALT WITH THE CANCER!

THE ONCOLOGIST WILL DISCUSS OPTIONS FOR ADJUVANT THERAPY AND HELP YOU DECIDE WHAT YOU WANT TO DO!

I WANT TO SURVIVE!

LES ... NOW THAT THE BANDAGES ARE OFF, DO YOU WANT TO SEE HOW... ?

OKAY, NOW REFRESH MY MEMORY ,... WHICH ONE WAS IT AGAIN ?

FWAAP!

SO? SO WHAT?

SO... DO YOU MISS MY...? SURE... A LITTLE...

BUT I'VE STILL GOT YOU!

4-7

THE ONCOLOGIST IS PROBABLY GOING TO SUGGEST CHEMOTHERAPY...

WHICH IS GOING TO MEAN YOU'LL LOSE YOUR HAIR, PUT ON WEIGHT, FEEL NAUSEATED AND TIRED, AND EXPERIENCE ACHES AND PAINS IN NEW PLACES!

PLEASE, HOLLY...YOU DON'T HAVE TO SUGARCOAT IT FOR ME!

4-8

HOW ARE THINGS WITH LES?
HE'S REALLY TRYING TO HELP AND HE SWEARS THE MASTECTOMY DOESN'T MAKE ANY DIFFERENCE!
IN FACT, HE LIKES TO DEAL WITH IT BY GETTING ME TO LAUGH ABOUT IT... BUT I WONDER HOW IT CAN'T CHANGE THINGS FOR HIM...
BATIUK
WHEN IT'S CHANGED SO MUCH FOR ME!
4-9

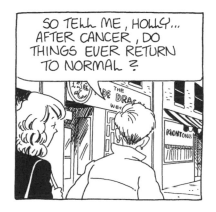

SO TELL ME, HOLLY... AFTER CANCER, DO THINGS EVER RETURN TO NORMAL?
MONTONES
MORE OR LESS... BUT EVENTUALLY YOU'LL COME TO REALIZE...
4-10
NORMAL ISN'T AS NORMAL AS IT ONCE WAS!
BATIUK

Two weeks later

IT LOOKS LIKE DR. HALLETT'S OFFICE IS ON THE FOURTH FLOOR!
Dr. Leslie Hallett
Oncologist - 4
IT'S AMAZING HOW MY LIFE HAS CHANGED!
LAST YEAR AT THIS TIME, I COULDN'T EVEN SPELL THE WORD ONCOLOGIST!
MEDICAL ARTS BUILDING
4-26
BATIUK

YOU'LL BE ON A CHEMOTHERAPY PROTOCOL KNOWN AS CA... WHICH CONSISTS OF THE DRUGS CYTOXAN AND ADRIAMYCIN!
EACH DRUG IS USUALLY GIVEN WITH THREE WEEKS ON AND ONE WEEK OFF... FOR A PERIOD OF SIX MONTHS OR SO!
4-27
WOW... IT LOOKS LIKE I'M REALLY GOING TO HAVE A REASON TO CELEBRATE COLUMBUS DAY THIS YEAR!
BATIUK

DO YOU HAVE ANY CHILDREN ?
NO... WHY ?
I WAS JUST GOING TO SAY THAT IF YOU'VE EVER BEEN PREGNANT...YOU'D FIND THAT CHEMO CAN SOMETIMES BE SIMILAR TO MORNING SICKNESS !
DR. LESLIE HALLETT
ONCOLOGIST
4-28
ACTUALLY... I HAVE HAD SOME EXPERIENCE WITH THAT !

I WAS THINKING ABOUT WHAT DR. HALLETT SAID ABOUT LISTENING TO SOOTHING MUSIC WHILE YOU'RE RECEIVING THE CHEMOTHERAPY ... SO I MADE YOU THIS TAPE !
4-29
'MUSIC FOR INJECTING POISONOUS CHEMICALS'... CATCHY !
ACTUALLY, I WAS THINKING OF CALLING IT 'WOODSTOCK III', BUT...

HOW IS LISA DOING WITH THE CHEMOTHERAPY?
WELL, I MADE DINNER FOR HER AFTER HER FIRST SESSION, AND SHE TOOK ONE LOOK AT IT AND THREW UP!
OPEN
I REMEMBER DOING THAT WHEN WE ROOMED TOGETHER AND YOU COOKED DINNER!
TRUE...
BATIUK
4-30

THE WORST THING ABOUT THE CHEMOTHERAPY IS THIS CONSTANT QUEASY FEELING!
I KNOW WHAT YOU NEED TO DO ... COME WITH ME!
BATIUK
5-1
GRANDMA ... LISA NEEDS YOUR HELP!

FUNKY WINKERBEAN
BY TOM BATIUK

GRANDMA'S KNOWLEDGE OF HERB HEALING COMES FROM FAMILY SECRETS THAT HAVE BEEN PASSED DOWN THROUGH THE AGES!

SHE CAN HELP YOU WITH THE SICKNESS FROM THE CHEMOTHERAPY AS WELL AS RESTORE YOUR BODY'S NATURAL CHI!

PLEASE SIT!

WE MUST ADDRESS THE IMBALANCE IN YOUR BODY... SO THAT YOUR BODY MAY REGAIN ITS NATURAL STATE!

YOU CAN TELL THIS BY TAKING MY PULSE?

NO... BY LISTENING TO YOUR PULSE!

DOCTORS TALK TO YOU ABOUT YOUR BODY...

BUT WITH GRANDMOTHER... YOUR BODY TALKS TO HER!

THESE HERBS WILL PERMIT YOUR CHI TO FLOW MORE FREELY!
CHI? FLOW?
YOU'LL STOP THROWING UP!
COUNT ME IN!
5-3

YOU MUST EAT ONLY FISH THAT SWIM IN RIVERS, AND ELIMINATE SPICY FOODS, ALCOHOL, AND SWEETS!
ALL SWEETS?
5-4
YOU KNOW WHAT THEY SAY ABOUT A LIFE THAT IS SWEET... IT IS SOMETIMES REGRETTABLY SHORT!

LIU LIN'S GRANDMOTHER SAID TO BOIL THESE HERBS AND THEN DRINK THE CONCOCTION TO RESTORE MY BODY'S NATURAL BALANCE!
SHE MUST KNOW SOMETHING ... SHE SMOKES LIKE A CHIMNEY, AND IS THE PICTURE OF HEALTH! NEITHER YOU NOR I SMOKE, AND WE BOTH ENDED UP WITH CANCER!
AND THEY SAY THE FATES HAVE NO SENSE OF HUMOR!
BATIUK
5-5

IT LOOKS LIKE MY BABE IS FEELING BETTER... SHE'S STARTED SUPPER!
HI, HONEY...THOSE HERBS I GOT FROM LIN'S GRANDMOTHER...
REALLY SEEM TO HELP WITH MY NAUSEA!
BATIUK
5-6

ARE YOU SURE YOU'RE REALLY UP TO THIS, LISA?
DON'T WORRY... WHEN I GET HOME FROM CLASS I'LL TAKE A LONG NAP!
BATIUK
5-7
HEY... DON'T FORGET YOUR SLIME SOUP!
OH... MY HERB WATER!

I MADE THIS MEAL FROM SUGGESTIONS THAT LIN'S GRANDMOTHER GAVE ME... I FIGURED IT WOULD DO US BOTH GOOD!
BATIUK
ASPARAGUS SOUP... GREEN TEA... BROCCOLI... MUSHROOMS... AND CANTALOUPE FOR DESSERT!
I NEED A PEPPERONI PIZZA AND I NEED IT **NOW!!**
MONTONI'S
Pizza
5-8

Four weeks after beginning chemotherapy

HOW IS LISA DOING WITH HER CHEMO, LES?
AMAZINGLY WELL, LINDA!
'SHE'S CARRYING A FULL LOAD OF CLASSES AT COMMUNITY COLLEGE AS IF NOTHING WAS WRONG!'
BATIUK
'FRANKLY, I DON'T KNOW HOW SHE DOES IT!'
5-24

BE SURE TO GET THESE IN SOME WATER RIGHT AWAY!
'BIG DATE TONIGHT?'
BATIUK
'YEP... IN FACT SHE'S PROBABLY GETTING READY RIGHT NOW!'
5-25

HEY, KIDDO... DID YOU FORGET ABOUT OUR 'DATE'?

I'M SORRY... BUT I'M JUST NOT IN THE MOOD!

THESE DAYS MY MIND MAKES DATES... BUT MY BODY KEEPS STANDING ME UP!

5-26

LOOK... IF YOU'RE NOT IN THE MOOD, LISA, THAT'S OKAY!

5-27

DR. HALLETT SAID THAT IT WAS IMPORTANT FOR YOU TO LISTEN TO YOUR BODY!

RIGHT NOW... YOU DON'T WANT TO HEAR THE LANGUAGE MY BODY IS USING!

HOW ABOUT IF YOU FIX YOURSELF SOMETHING TO EAT... I'M GOING TO LIE DOWN!
5-28
THAT'S GOOD... DR. HALLETT SAID THAT THE BEST THING FOR YOU WAS TO DRINK PLENTY OF FLUIDS AND REST!
I'VE GOT NEWS FOR YOU... THEY'RE MUTUALLY EXCLUSIVE!

LISTEN... IF THERE'S ANYTHING I CAN DO...
I JUST WANT TO BE ALONE! I'M DISFIGURED, EXHAUSTED, GOING BALD AND GAINING WEIGHT...!
5-29
WHAT DO YOU WANT FROM ME!?
SLAM!
I WANT THINGS LIKE THEY WERE!

HI... FUNKY SAID YOU DIDN'T FEEL UP TO WORKING TODAY AND I THOUGHT YOU COULD USE A LITTLE PICK-ME-UP!

I'S

LIKE WHAT?

THE ONE THAT ALWAYS WORKS FOR ME...

5-31

SHOPPING!!

GOING TO THE MALL IS A SWEET IDEA, CINDY...BUT I'M NOT IN THE MOOD TO HAVE THE WORLD SEE HOW GROSS I'M STARTING TO LOOK!

6-1

THAT'S JUST THE POINT... NOTHING CAN LIFT A GIRL'S SPIRITS LIKE COMING ACROSS A GREAT M D F!

AN M D F?

A 'MARKED DOWN FROM'!

ONE OF THE THINGS I WANT TO TAKE YOU SHOPPING FOR IS A WIG!
OH, NO... I DON'T THINK SO! I'M IN A LOUSY MOOD ALREADY AND THAT WOULD BE JUST TOO DEPRESSING!
6-2
THERE ARE NO BUMMERS SHOPPING WITH SUMMERS!
BATIUK

I DID A STORY FOR CHANNEL SEVEN ON RENOIR'S ... AND ONE OF THE THINGS THEY SPECIALIZE IN IS WIGS FOR WOMEN WHO ARE UNDERGOING CHEMO!
Renoir's
SALON
I DON'T THINK SO ... WITH THESE BAGS UNDER MY EYES, IT MAKES ME LOOK LIKE WILLIE NELSON!
6-3
BATIUK

I DON'T THINK SO...
BATIUK
THERE'S ONLY ROOM FOR ONE BLOND BOMBER IN THIS TOWN!
6-4

WHAT DO YOU THINK?
YOU LOOK STUNNING!
Renoir's
SALON
BATIUK
6-5

HOW'S LISA DOING, LES?
SHE'S GOING THROUGH KIND OF A TOUGH TIME WITH HER CHEMO, NATE... EACH TIME I GO HOME THESE DAYS...
'I NEVER KNOW WHAT TO EXPECT!'
BATIUK
6-8

WELCOME HOME...
BATIUK
6-9
LET'S MISBEHAVE...
MY HAIR'S ALL GONE...
BURMA SHAVE!

DO YOU LIKE MY NEW WIG?
IT LOOKS GREAT! IN FACT, YOU LOOK GREAT! NOT ONLY THAT... YOU LOOK...
MONTONI'S Pizza
MONTONI'S PIZZA
CINDY FOUND A NEW USE FOR THOSE OLD SHOULDER PADS OF MINE!
BATIUK
6-10

CINDY TOOK ME SHOPPING... SHE SAID A NEW LOOK WOULD GIVE ME A NEW OUTLOOK...
AND YOU KNOW WHAT?
BATIUK
6-11
IT WORKED!

THANKS AGAIN, CINDY... I REALLY APPRECIATE WHAT YOU DID!
6-12

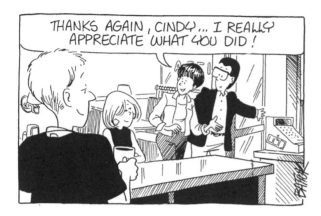

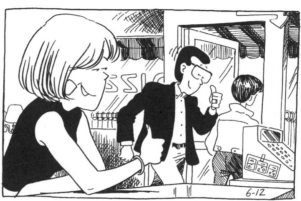

FUNKY WINKERBEAN
by TOM BATIUK
MONTONI'S Pizza
MONTONI'S PIZZA
YOU MEAN TO TELL ME THERE AREN'T ANY MORE BASKETBALL GAMES LEFT?
I THINK OUR CONSTITUTIONAL RIGHTS TO WATCH A BASKETBALL GAME ARE BEING VIOLATED!
IF YOU'RE LOOKING FOR SOMETHING TO DO... YOU COULD ALWAYS SNUGGLE WITH YOUR WIFE!
AN EXCELLENT IDEA!
I LOVE YOUR HAIR, BY THE WAY... WHERE DO YOU HAVE IT DONE?
HONG KONG!

One year later

WHILE I'M ON SPRING BREAK FROM SCHOOL... I THOUGHT THAT MAYBE I COULD HELP YOU WADE THROUGH SOME OF THE REMAINING INSURANCE PAPERWORK FROM MY BREAST CANCER TREATMENTS!
GREAT! IT'S ALL CAREFULLY FILED AWAY IN THIS MANILA FOLDER...
4-17
AND THIS MANILA FOLDER... AND THIS MANILA FOLDER...

ARE ALL OF THESE FOLDERS FILLED WITH HOSPITAL BILLS?
NOT EXACTLY...
THIS ONE IS FOR STATEMENTS... THIS ONE IS FOR INVOICES... THIS THIN ONE IS FOR BILLS THAT WERE PAID BY OUR HEALTH PLAN, DENIALCARE...
4-18
AND THIS ONE IS FOR THE ONES THAT I COULDN'T FIGURE OUT!

FIRST THE HOSPITAL SENDS US A BILL TELLING US WHAT DENIALCARE HAS PAID AND WHAT WE HAVE TO PAY!

AFTER WE'VE PAID THAT... THEY SEND US A BILL FOR THE AMOUNT THAT THEY SAID DENIALCARE HAD PAID!

AND THEN A FEW MONTHS AFTER THAT, THEY SEND US A BILL FOR THE ENTIRE AMOUNT!

OKAY, SO NOW WHAT DO YOU DO WITH THIS LAST PILE OF STATEMENTS FROM THE HOSPITAL?

THE ONES THAT WE CAN'T FIGURE OUT IF WE'RE SUPPOSED TO PAY OR NOT?

YEAH...

I USUALLY JUST LET THOSE GO UNTIL WE GET AN OVERDUE PAYMENT NOTICE!

IT SAYS HERE THAT OUR HEALTHCARE PROVIDER, DENIALCARE, HAS SWITCHED US TO A 'POINT OF SERVICE PLAN'!

WHAT EXACTLY DOES THAT MEAN?

IT MEANS THAT WHENEVER WE FILE A CLAIM...

WE GET A LETTER FROM THEM SAYING THAT THEY DON'T SEE THE POINT OF THAT SERVICE!

4-21

WHY WAS I CHARGED TWICE FOR RADIATION TREATMENTS ON THE SAME DAY?

WHEN I CHECKED INTO THAT, THEY SAID THAT THEY HAD DISCOVERED SOME FAULTY SHIELDING ON ONE OF THE MACHINES IN THE RADIATION LAB...

4-22

SO THEY SENT BILLS TO PEOPLE WHO HAD BEEN IN ADJOINING ROOMS!

FUNKY WINKERBEAN
by TOM BATIUK
WA...
HOO !!
I FINALLY FIGURED OUT THIS MAZE OF HOSPITAL BILLING FORMS !
ALL THAT'S LEFT IS THIS LETTER THAT CAME TODAY FROM THE HOSPITAL !
'DEAR PATIENT... WE WANT TO INFORM YOU THAT WE'RE CONVERTING TO A NEW BILLING SYSTEM...'
AAUUUUUUGGGHH!!

HOW IS LISA DOING THESE DAYS, LES ?
SHE'S DOING GREAT !
I THINK SHE'S FINALLY REACHED A POINT WHERE SHE'S MANAGED TO PUT ALL THOUGHTS OF CANCER BEHIND HER !
BATIUK
AND IT'S LIKE I LIVE MY LIFE THESE DAYS WAITING FOR THE OTHER SHOE TO DROP !
JITTERS
6-5

EVERY MORNING WHEN I STEP OUT OF THE SHOWER AND LOOK IN THE MIRROR... I'M REMINDED OF THE CANCER !
JITTERS
6-6
AND YOU WANT TO KNOW WHEN YOU CAN FINALLY GO BACK TO A HAPPILY UNAWARE EXISTENCE !
EXACTLY !
YOU CAN'T !

MENU
MENU
BATIUK
ARE YOU OKAY ?
WOMEN
6-7

BATIUK
YES ... MY NAME IS LISA MOORE ...
MEN
6-8
AND I'D LIKE TO MAKE AN APPOINTMENT TO SEE THE DOCTOR !

ALL RIGHT... WHAT'S GOING ON?
WHAT DO YOU MEAN?
6-9
YOU CLEANED THE APARTMENT LAST NIGHT... AND NOW YOU'RE CLEANING IT AGAIN THIS MORNING!
BATIUK
SOMETHING'S GOING ON!

SO GIVE IT UP, LEESE... WHAT'S GOING ON?
I'VE MADE AN APPOINTMENT WITH A SURGEON!
BATIUK
6-10
I THINK I WANT TO HAVE RECONSTRUCTIVE SURGERY!

I'VE BEEN THINKING MORE AND MORE ABOUT HAVING RECONSTRUCTIVE BREAST SURGERY!
BATIUK
6-12
I REALLY HATE THIS PROSTHESIS THAT I HAVE TO WEAR!
THE OTHER DAY IN MONTONI'S I HAD TO REACH UP TO PUT SOMETHING ON A SHELF AND THE BLEEPING THING POPPED OUT!

I NEVER REALIZED THAT THE PROSTHESIS YOU'VE WORN IN YOUR BRA SINCE YOUR CANCER SURGERY WAS SUCH A NUISANCE!
BATIUK
I GUESS IT WOULD BE NICE TO BE ABLE TO HUG SOMEONE WITHOUT BEING AFRAID THAT THEY'LL BOUNCE OFF!
6-13

THE WOMEN'S HEALTH AND CANCER RIGHTS ACT REQUIRES THAT INSURANCE COMPANIES PAY FOR BREAST RECONSTRUCTION!

SO EVEN OUR HMO, DENIALCARE, WOULD HAVE TO PAY FOR IT!

JUST REMEMBER... YOU DON'T HAVE TO DO IT FOR ME!

I KNOW... I WANT TO DO IT FOR ME!

NOW WHEN IT COMES TO IMPLANTS... SMALL-BREASTED WOMEN SUCH AS YOURSELF DO QUITE WELL...

IT'S JUST ONE HUMILIATION AFTER ANOTHER...

ALTHOUGH WE CAN ALSO RECONSTRUCT THE BREAST WITH TISSUE FROM THE ABDOMEN, BACK OR BUTTOCK AREA!

ALTHOUGH, WHAT'S ONE MORE POUND ON AN ELEPHANT?

63

I WANT YOU TO LOOK AT SOME PICTURES AND DISCUSS IMPLANT SIZES... BUT FIRST I WANT TO TAKE SOME MEASUREMENTS!

I'D SAY YOU'RE ABOUT A 34 A...?

ON A GOOD DAY!

6-16

SAY, THOSE ARE NICE!

DR. WOLLMAN
PLASTIC SURGEON

TRY NOT TO ENJOY THIS SO MUCH!

6-17

SORRY... I GUESS I WAS JUST FLASHING BACK TO MY COLLEGE DORM-ROOM DAYS!

OUR HMO, DENIALCARE, HAS AGREED TO PAY FOR MY RECONSTRUCTIVE SURGERY... SO WHY AREN'T I HAPPY ABOUT IT ?
6-19
I KNEW THAT YOU CAN EXPERIENCE A LETDOWN AFTER CHEMO IS OVER...
BUT I FIGURED THAT EVENTUALLY I'D BE LET BACK UP !
BATIUK

I NEVER DREAMED THAT MY LIFE WOULD TURN OUT LIKE THIS !
BATIUK
6-20
I GUESS THAT'S THE PROBLEM WITH DREAMS... THEY NEVER INCLUDE COMPLICATIONS...
AND A LIFE WITHOUT COMPLICATIONS JUST DOESN'T EXIST !

NO MATTER HOW GOOD THE RECONSTRUCTIVE SURGERY IS ... THINGS WILL NEVER BE THE SAME!
I'D ALWAYS PICTURED MYSELF HAVING CHILDREN AND NURSING THEM...
WESTVIEW PARK
HOW DO YOU EXPLAIN TO A BABY THAT THE OTHER ONE IS JUST FOR SHOW?
6-21
BATIUK

I NEVER HAD A MODEL'S FIGURE ... BUT I ALWAYS LIKED MY BODY AND FELT GOOD ABOUT HOW I LOOKED!
WESTVIEW
6-22
WHAT IS IT ABOUT GOD THAT MAKES HIM HATE PRIDE SO MUCH...
WHILE BEING SO INDIFFERENT TO SUFFERING?
BATIUK

MAYBE IT'S TIME FOR ME TO REALIZE THAT I CAN'T CONTROL EVERYTHING THAT'S GOING TO HAPPEN...

AND THAT THE BEST THING TO DO IS THROW THE SCRIPT AWAY...

6-23

AND JUST LET THE PLAY UNFOLD!

HEY, KID... WHAT HAVE YOU BEEN UP TO?

OH, JUST OUT WALKING AND LEARNING ABOUT LIFE!

6-24

AND YOU LEARNED...?

THAT LIFE ISN'T A WALK IN THE PARK...

BUT THAT FACT SHOULDN'T KEEP YOU FROM ENJOYING A WALK IN THE PARK!

WHAT MADE YOU DECIDE TO GO INTO PLASTIC SURGERY?
I LIKE KNOWING THAT MY PATIENTS WILL BE AROUND TO ENJOY MY WORK!
6-26
BATIUK

YOUR WIFE CAME THROUGH THE SURGERY JUST FINE AND SHE'S RESTING COMFORTABLY!
UHHHHH....
6-27
BATIUK

I CAN'T BELIEVE THEY'RE SENDING ME HOME IN THIS CONDITION!
621
BATIUK
DENIALCARE, OUR HMO, WILL ONLY PAY FOR YOU TO STAY IN THE HOSPITAL ONE DAY!
IF I'M NOT SICK ENOUGH TO BE IN A HOSPITAL... I WONDER WHO IS?
6-28

I'M REALLY PLEASED WITH THE RESULT... HERE, TAKE A LOOK!
BATIUK
6-29
I WONDER IF HE'D FEEL BAD IF I SCREAMED?

I THINK DR. WOLLMAN DID A GREAT JOB WITH THE RECONSTRUCTION!

THEN WHY ARE YOU SQUINTING?

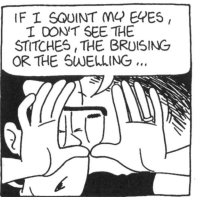

IF I SQUINT MY EYES, I DON'T SEE THE STITCHES, THE BRUISING OR THE SWELLING...

I JUST SEE SOMEONE I LOVE!

6-30

THANKS FOR LOVING ME EVEN IN MY BRUISED AND BATTERED RECONSTRUCTED CONDITION!

HUBBA HUBBA!

7-1

YOU'RE PATHETIC!

70

SO DOES LISA HAVE A CLASS TONIGHT, LES ?
NO... ACTUALLY, TONIGHT'S THE NIGHT THAT HER CLUB MEETS...
10-16
I'D LIKE TO WELCOME A NEW MEMBER THIS EVENING TO OUR BREAST CANCER SUPPORT GROUP...

WHEN I WENT THROUGH CHEMO, I FOUND THERE WERE TWO THINGS I NEEDED MORE THAN ANYTHING ELSE...
WESTVIEW COMMUNITY CENTER
A LOT OF LOVE AND NAPS...
MOSTLY NAPS !
10-17

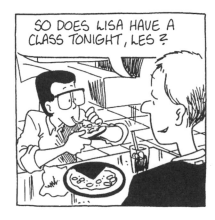

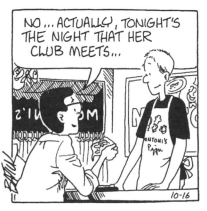

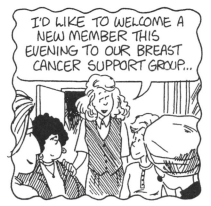

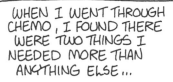

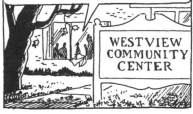

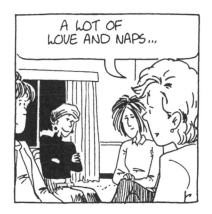

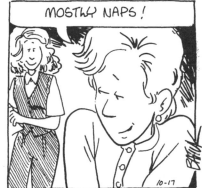

SINCE I'VE BEEN ON CHEMO... OUR FRIENDS AND RELATIVES HAVE PROVIDED MEALS ALMOST EVERY NIGHT...

AND MY HUSBAND HAS BEEN SO WONDERFUL HELPING WITH THE HOUSEWORK AND THE KIDS!

10-18

I'M ALMOST GOING TO HATE TO SEE THE CHEMO END!

I DON'T HAVE A HUSBAND OR A BOYFRIEND AT THE MOMENT... BUT I DO HAVE A CAT...

Breast Cancer Support Group 7:30

10-19

AND I'VE LEARNED THAT CATS DON'T FRET ABOUT THE PAST OR WORRY ABOUT WHAT MIGHT HAPPEN IN THE FUTURE... THEY JUST EXIST IN THE MOMENT, AND IT MADE ME REALIZE THAT TODAY IS CALLED 'THE PRESENT'...

BECAUSE IT'S A GIFT!

IF ANYONE WOULD LIKE TO MODEL WIGS AND CLOTHING IN OUR BREAST CANCER FASHION SHOW NEXT WEEK ... SEE ME AT THE END OF THE MEETING!
IF THIS IS WHAT IT TAKES TO BREAK INTO MODELING ... YOU CAN HAVE IT!
10-20

DON'T FORGET THAT IF YOU CAN'T MAKE IT TO OUR SUPPORT GROUP MEETING ...
WESTVIEW COMMUNITY CENTER
10-21
THERE'S A LOCAL BREAST CANCER CHAT ROOM THAT YOU CAN ACCESS ON THE INTERNET!
IS THERE AN UNBURDENING, UNLOADING, LET-IT-ALL-HANG-OUT ROOM?

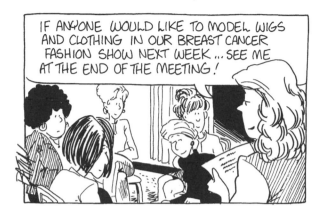

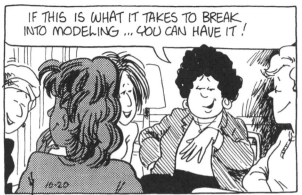

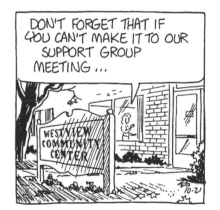

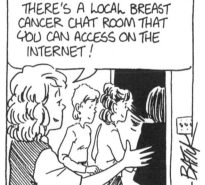

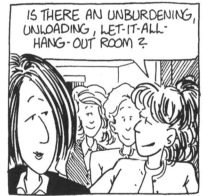

I WAS WONDERING IF OUR BREAST CANCER SUPPORT GROUP COULD RESERVE A ROOM HERE IN MONTONI'S FOR OUR MONTHLY MEETING?

NO PROBLEM, LISA... DO YOU WANT SMOKING OR NON?

5-3

NON, PLEASE... WE'VE ALREADY HAD CANCER.

OUR FIRST ORDER OF BUSINESS AT THIS MONTH'S BREAST CANCER SUPPORT GROUP MEETING...

IS TO PRESENT LISA MOORE WITH HER FIVE-YEAR SURVIVOR PIN.

5-4

CONGRATULATIONS!

THANKS... ALTHOUGH THIS IS A HECK OF A WAY TO COLLECT JEWELRY.

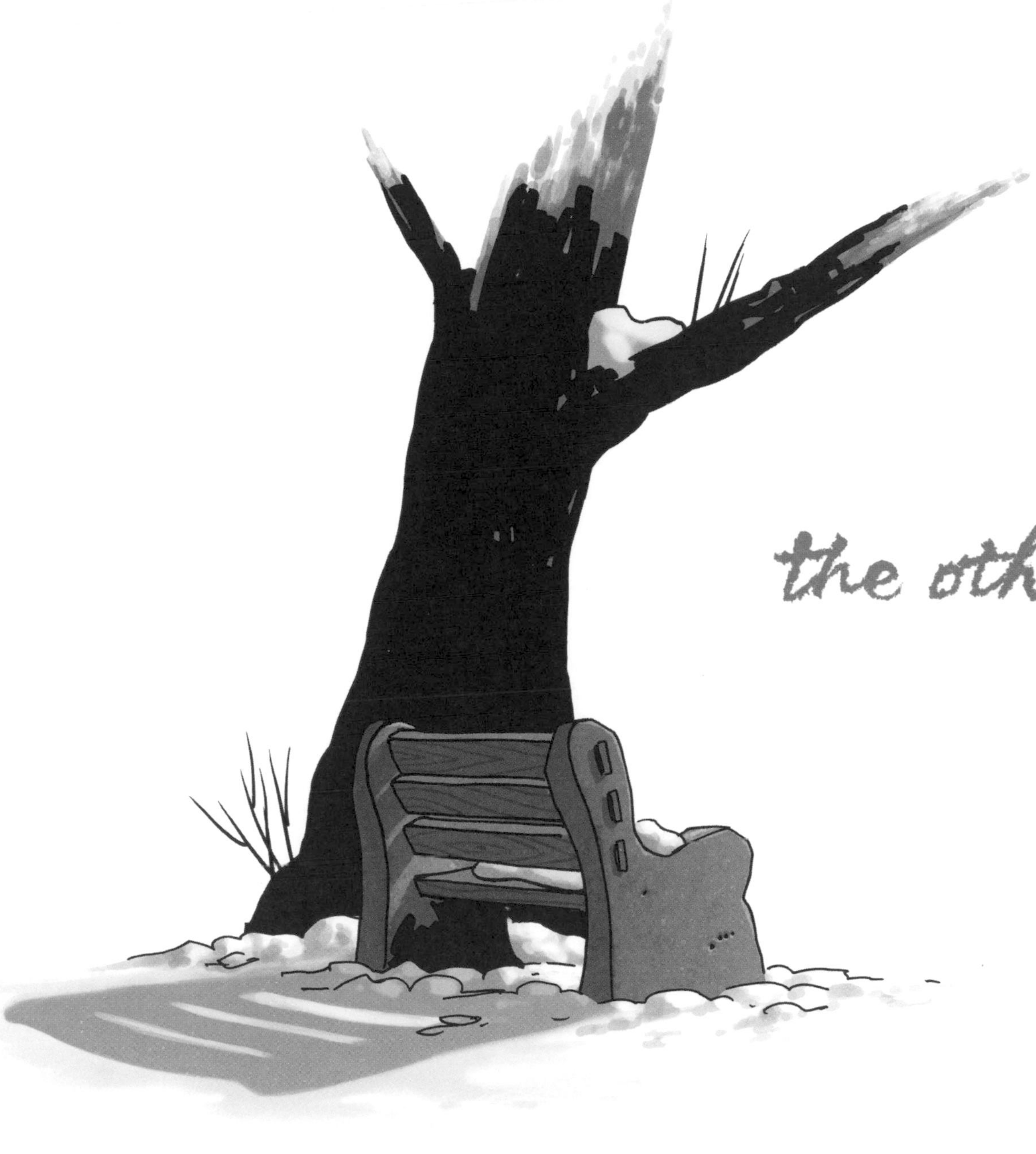

the other shoe

Seven years later

IT WAS A GOOD IDEA TO GET TOGETHER TONIGHT WHILE LISA AND HOLLY ARE AT THEIR BREAST CANCER SUPPORT GROUP MEETING.

YEAH...THERE'S NOTHING LIKE AN EVENING OF BABYSITTING AND MALE BONDING.

2-27

I SEE WE HAVE SOME NEW FACES AT OUR MEETING TONIGHT...

SO I'D LIKE TO TELL YOU A LITTLE BIT ABOUT OUR BREAST CANCER SUPPORT GROUP.

WESTVIEW COMMUNITY CENTER

2-28

ONE OF THE THINGS WE DO IS TO HOLD FUND-RAISERS FOR BREAST CANCER RESEARCH.

IT'S SORT OF LIKE A MEMBERSHIP DRIVE IN REVERSE.

ALONG WITH OTHER BREAST CANCER SUPPORT GROUPS, WE'RE TAKING PART IN A GENE RESEARCH STUDY THAT'S LOOKING FOR GENETIC MARKERS FOR BREAST CANCER.
IF SUCH A MARKER COULD BE FOUND, IT WOULD NOT ONLY HELP WITH EARLY DETECTION...
BUT WOULD ALSO GIVE YOU ONE MORE THING TO BE UPSET WITH YOUR MOTHER ABOUT.
3-1

AGAIN, FOR THE NEW LADIES IN OUR BREAST CANCER SUPPORT GROUP...
I WANT TO SAY IT'S NOT YOUR FAULT!
SUPPORT GROUP NOTES
NOT SMOKING, EATING RIGHT AND EXERCISING ARE ALL GOOD THINGS TO DO IF YOU WANT TO AVOID CANCER...
UNFORTUNATELY, CANCER DOESN'T GIVE A ★#@!
3-2

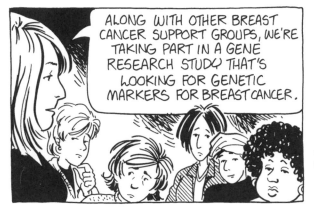

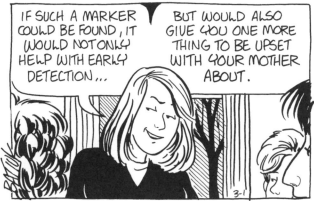

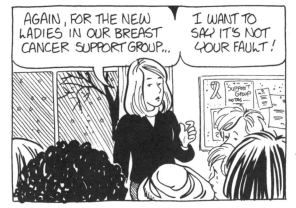

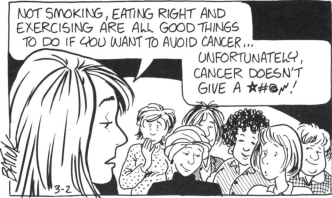

IT DOESN'T MATTER IF YOU'RE A SUPERMARKET CLERK OR A SUPER MODEL...

THE COLD FEAR THAT YOU FEEL WHEN YOU'RE TOLD YOU HAVE CANCER...

ISN'T DIMINISHED BY YOUR INCOME OR STATUS IN LIFE...

LIKE I SAID...

WESTVIEW COMMUNITY

3-3

CANCER DOESN'T GIVE A ✴#☉!!

YOU GUYS ARE QUICK STUDIES.

AS YOU'VE JUST SHOWN...

LAUGHTER CAN BE A PRETTY STRONG MEDICINE FOR DEALING WITH CANCER.

3-4

IF LAUGHTER IS GOOD MEDICINE, THEN I'M IN GREAT SHAPE...

BECAUSE MY HMO IS A JOKE.

FUNKY WINKERBEAN by Tom Batiuk

WESTVIEW COMMUNITY CENTER

ARE THERE ANY MORE QUESTIONS BEFORE WE WRAP UP THIS MEETING OF OUR BREAST CANCER SUPPORT GROUP?

DOES THE FEAR EVER GO AWAY?

NOT COMPLETELY.

WE ALL KNOW WE'RE GOING TO DIE EVENTUALLY...

3-5

BUT IT'S LIKE SITTING ON A PLANE READING A MAGAZINE AS THE ATTENDANT EXPLAINS WHERE THE NEAREST EXIT IS.

YOU'RE VAGUELY AWARE THAT SOMETHING BAD COULD HAPPEN, BUT IT DOESN'T REALLY REGISTER.

AFTER YOU'VE HAD CANCER...YOU KNOW WHERE THE EXIT IS...

AND NO AMOUNT OF TRYING TO GO BACK TO THE WAY THINGS WERE KEEPS YOU FROM KNOWING.

I DIDN'T REALIZE YOU'D HAVE TO DRAW BLOOD FOR THIS GENE RESEARCH STUDY.
I'M SORRY... DOES THE SIGHT OF BLOOD MAKE YOU QUEASY?
JUST MY OWN.
3-20

YOU'RE VERY GOOD... I BARELY EVEN FELT THAT.
THANKS ... IT'S NICE TO GET A COMPLIMENT ONCE IN A WHILE ...
INSTEAD OF...'IS THIS YOUR FIRST DAY?'
3-21

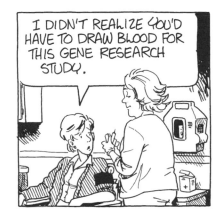

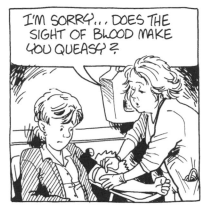

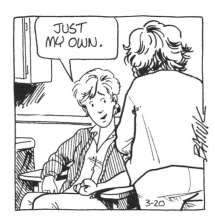

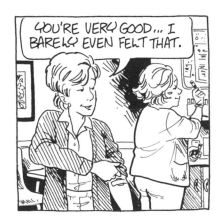

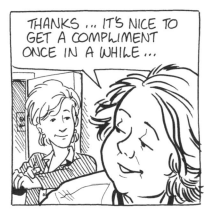

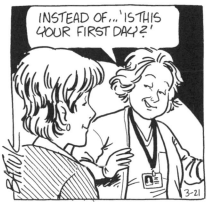

I APPRECIATE 'REACH TO RECOVERY' HAVING YOU STOP BY.
NO PROBLEM ... IN FACT I WAS ALREADY HERE TODAY TO TAKE PART IN A RESEARCH STUDY.
RN - STACY
LRN - ANNE
DO YOU EVER STOP THINKING ABOUT IT?
NOT COMPLETELY...
BUT ONE MORNING YOU WAKE UP AND IT'S NOT THE FIRST THING YOU THINK OF.
3-22

ONE LAST QUESTION ...
HOW DO YOU DEAL WITH THE FEAR?
23
BY TAKING IT ONE DAY AT A TIME.
IT'S ALL ABOUT INHALING AND EXHALING.
3-23

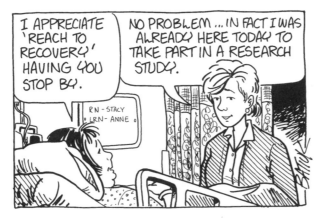

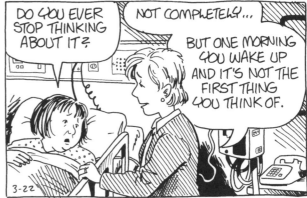

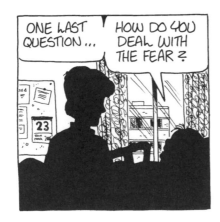

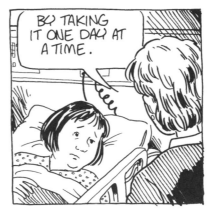

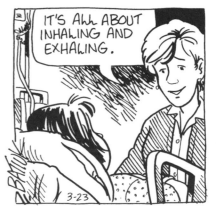

YES, THIS IS LISA...
THE GENE RESEARCH STUDY?
LISA MOORE ATTORNEY AT LAW
SURE, I COULD COME IN FOR MORE TESTS...
BATIUK
3-24

WE SHOULD HAVE THE RESULTS FOR YOU BY NEXT WEEK.
ACTUALLY, MY HUSBAND AND I WERE ABOUT TO LEAVE FOR A VACATION OVER HIS SPRING BREAK.
3-25
BATIUK
THAT'S FINE... JUST GIVE US A CALL BEFORE YOU LEAVE.
BUT DON'T FORGET.
YOU'RE KIDDING RIGHT?

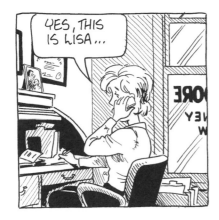

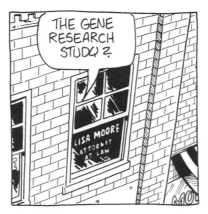

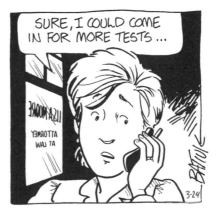

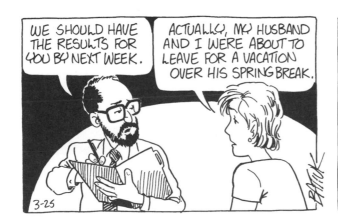

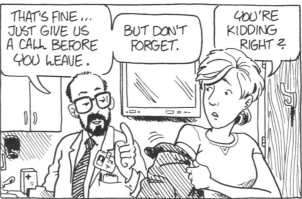

FUNKY WINKERBEAN
by TOM BATIUK
YOWEE!!
THE NEW YORKER MAGAZINE IS HOLDING ONE OF THE SHORT STORIES I SENT THEM, SUMMER!!
WHAT DAY IS THIS!?
I'M GOING TO CIRCLE MARCH 26TH AND FROM THIS DAY FORWARD IT WILL OFFICIALLY BE KNOWN AS "DADDY'S BIG DAY"!
3-26
IN FACT, I FEEL SO GOOD RIGHT NOW I'M GOING TO CELEBRATE BY DOING MY HAPPY DANCE!
HAPPY DANCE!
BATIUK
WHAT?
WHAT?

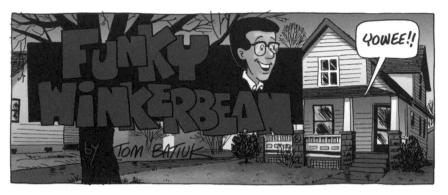

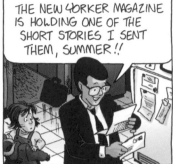

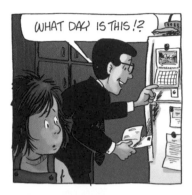

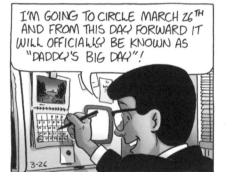

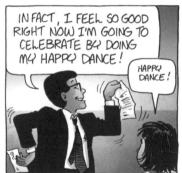

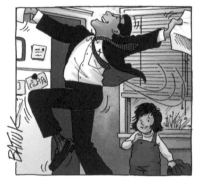

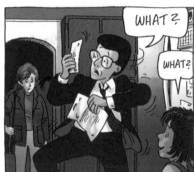

APPARENTLY THEY NOTICED SOMETHING WHEN THEY DID THE BLOODWORK.

AND THEY CALLED AND ASKED ME TO COME IN FOR MORE TESTS.

LEESE... I WISH I HAD A SCRIPT FOR THIS SO I'D KNOW WHAT TO SAY NEXT.

THANKS FOR BRINGING US HERE.

THERE'S JUST SOMETHING ABOUT THE BOOTHS, THE BAR, AND THE BANDBOX THAT MAKES ME FEEL SAFE...

NO MATTER HOW WORRIED I MAY BE.

YOU KNOW ... LIFE WOULD BE PRETTY SWEET IF IT WASN'T FOR HAVING TO DEAL WITH THE OCCASIONAL @#★N*!

3-29

@#★N*!

MY BAD.

WHATEVER THE RESULTS OF THE TEST ARE... WE'LL DEAL WITH IT.

3-30

YOU KNOW HOW MUCH I LOVE YOU?

UP TO THE STARS AND BACK?

AND AROUND VENUS TWO TIMES AND BACK.

I'M CALLING TO CHECK ON THE RESULTS OF MY TEST.
20
BATIUK
I'M AFRAID THE RESULTS WERE POSITIVE... YOUR CANCER HAS METASTASIZED.
WE'LL TALK WHEN YOU GET BACK.
HAVE A NICE VACATION.
3-31

HE SAID THE RESULTS WERE POSITIVE AND THAT THE CANCER HAS RETURNED.
BATIUK
HE WANTS ME TO CALL WHEN WE GET BACK.
IF ONLY THIS WERE SOME KIND OF APRIL FOOL'S JOKE.
4-1

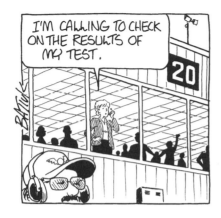

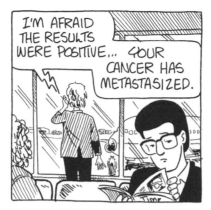

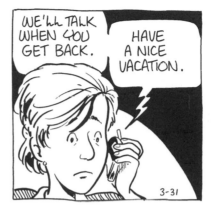

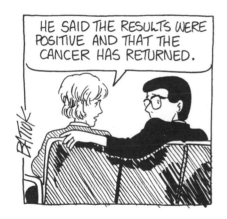

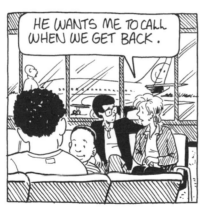

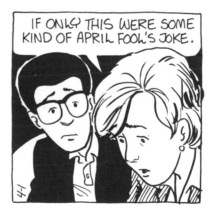

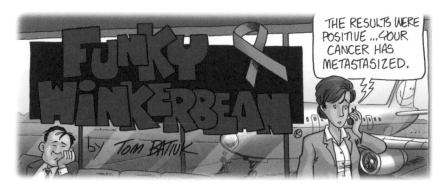

FUNKY WINKERBEAN
by TOM BATIUK
THE RESULTS WERE POSITIVE ...YOUR CANCER HAS METASTASIZED.
4-2
I CAN'T BELIEVE THIS IS HAPPENING.
BATIUK

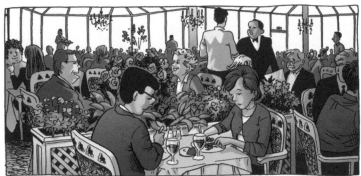

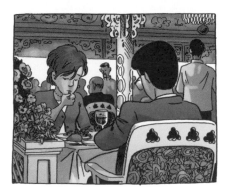

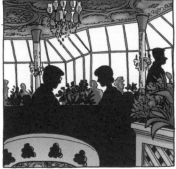

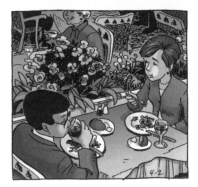

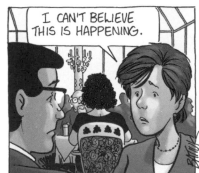

DO YOU WANT TO GO ON A CARRIAGE RIDE THROUGH THE PARK?
THAT'S SWEET, BUT THAT COSTS SO MUCH, AND WE'D BETTER START WATCHING OUR PENNIES...
4-3
WE DON'T CALL OUR HMO 'DENIAL CARE' FOR NOTHING.

I DON'T GET IT, LEESE...
YOU'VE BEEN ALMOST SEVEN YEARS CANCER FREE.
4-4
YOUR CANCER SHOULDN'T BE COMING BACK NOW.
APPARENTLY THE CANCER HAD OTHER IDEAS.
STRAWBERRY FIELDS

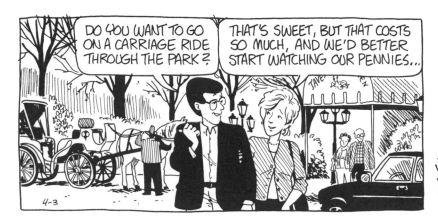

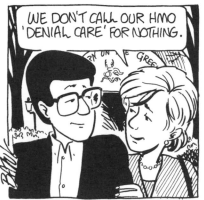

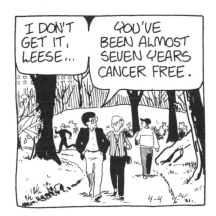

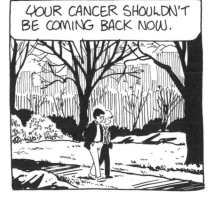

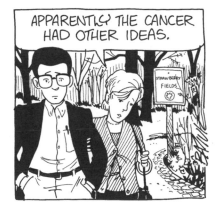

WITH EACH YEAR THAT PASSED FOLLOWING MY BREAST CANCER SURGERY I BEGAN FEELING MORE AND MORE SAFE.

4-5

I JUST NEVER SAW THE SECOND SHOOTER...

I SUPPOSE I CAN STOP TAKING THE TAMOXIFEN NOW.

I NEED TO FOCUS ON SOMETHING OTHER THAN CANCER.

I WONDER WHAT THOSE LITTLE PLAQUES ON THE BENCHES ARE FOR?

IN MEMORY OF MY BELOVED DOTTIE WHO LOVED THE PARK

4-6

THAT DIDN'T HELP...

NO...

DARIN SEEMS TO HAVE A BAD CASE OF SPRING FEVER...
LES SAID HE WAS IN ANOTHER TIME ZONE YESTERDAY.
OFFICE
SPEAKING OF LES... HE'S TAKING A PERSONAL DAY.
APPARENTLY LISA'S CANCER HAS RETURNED.
LIFE JUST #★@*s!
NO... SOMETIMES LIFE JUST #★@*S.
MEDICA
OFFI
5-8

I'D LIKE TO KNOW WHAT TESTS YOU'VE HAD SO FAR.
ALL OF THEM?
YES.
HOW MUCH TIME HAVE YOU GOT?
5-9

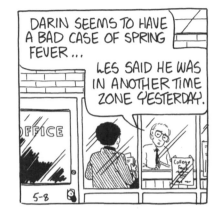

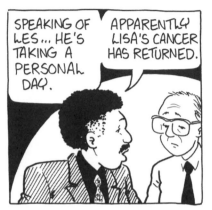

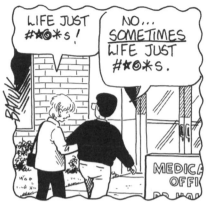

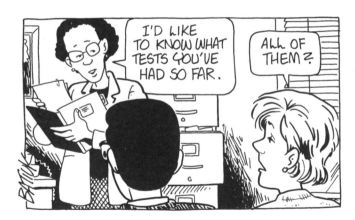

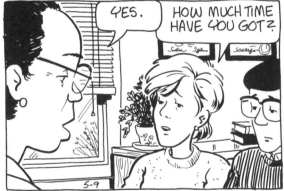

A WOMAN WHO HAD NEGATIVE NODES AND A SMALL CANCER...

THE STATISTICS SAY THAT EIGHTY PERCENT OF THEM WILL BE LONG-TERM SURVIVORS.

5-10

UNFORTUNATELY, FOR REASONS WE DON'T FULLY COMPREHEND...TWENTY PERCENT OF THOSE CANCERS WILL RECUR.

MY WHOLE LIFE I'VE WANTED TO BE UNIQUE AND STAND APART FROM THE CROWD...

AND WHERE DOES IT HAPPEN?

METASTATIC BREAST CANCER IS NOT REGARDED AS A CURABLE DISEASE.

THE IDEA IS TO STRETCH THINGS OUT AS FAR AS YOU CAN.

DO YOU HAVE ANY QUESTIONS?

I DON'T EVEN KNOW WHERE TO START...

5-11

I UNDERSTAND,

OFTEN PATIENTS WANT TO KNOW HOW LONG...

NOT AN OPTION...

I WAS KIND OF LOOKING FORWARD TO A MIDLIFE CRISIS.

I'M SORRY... I JUST NEED A FEW MINUTES TO PROCESS ALL OF THIS.
I KNOW...
BATIUK
TAKE AS LONG AS YOU NEED.
5-12

BATIUK
5-13
DR. HALLETT
ONCOLOGIST

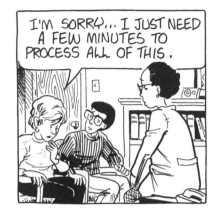

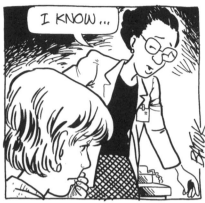

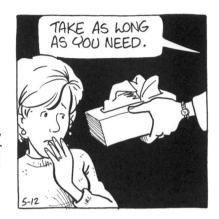

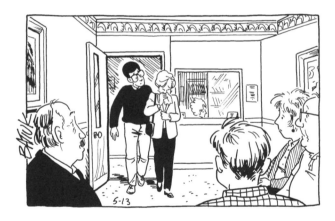

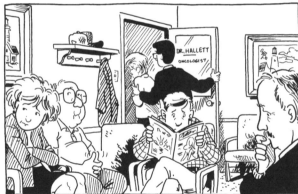

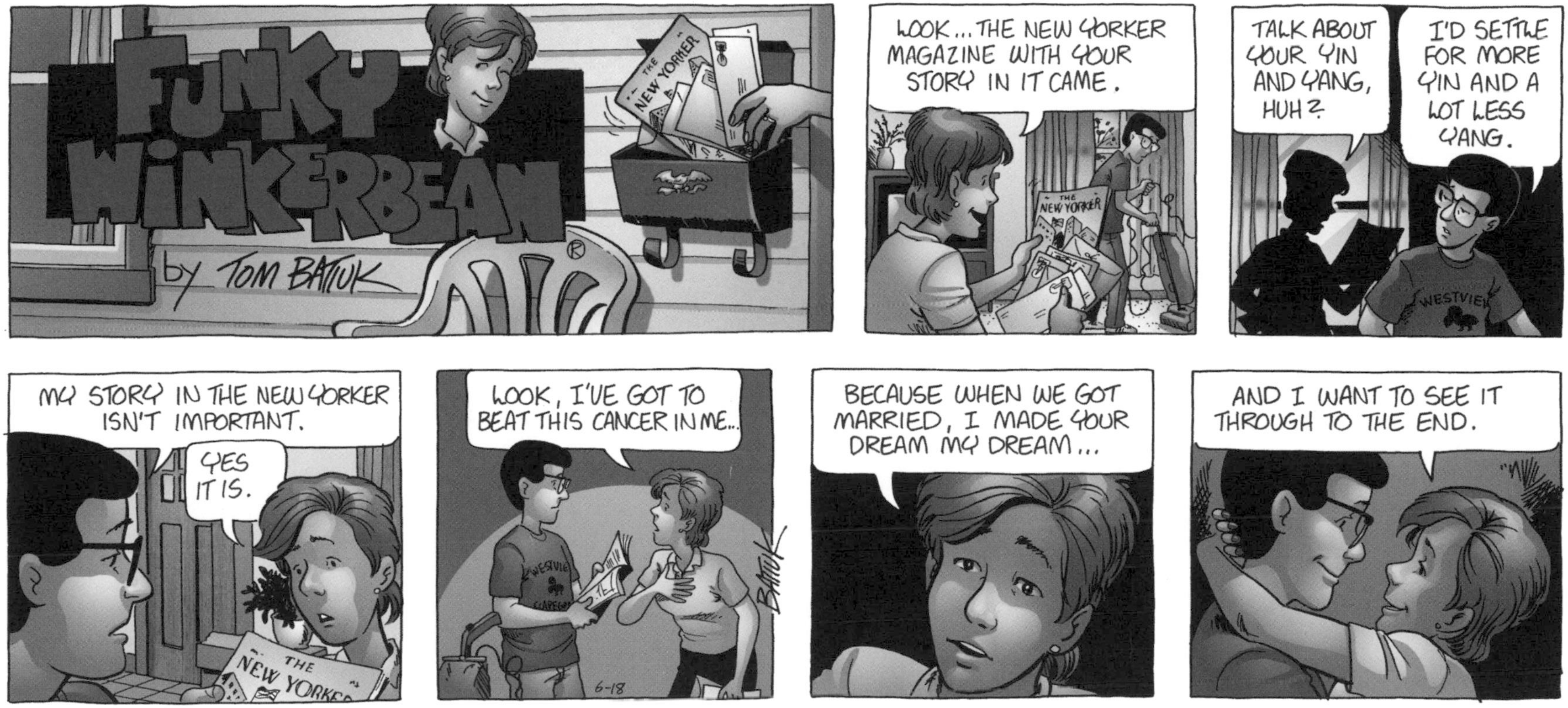
FUNKY WINKERBEAN
by TOM BATIUK
THE NEW YORKER
LOOK... THE NEW YORKER MAGAZINE WITH YOUR STORY IN IT CAME.
THE NEW YORKER
TALK ABOUT YOUR YIN AND YANG, HUH?
I'D SETTLE FOR MORE YIN AND A LOT LESS YANG.
WESTVIEW
MY STORY IN THE NEW YORKER ISN'T IMPORTANT.
YES IT IS.
THE NEW YORKER
LOOK, I'VE GOT TO BEAT THIS CANCER IN ME...
BATIUK
6-18
BECAUSE WHEN WE GOT MARRIED, I MADE YOUR DREAM MY DREAM...
AND I WANT TO SEE IT THROUGH TO THE END.

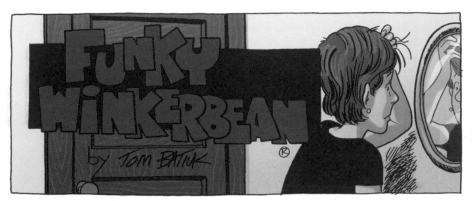

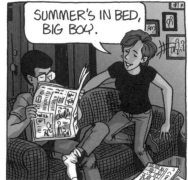

FUNKY WINKERBEAN
by TOM BATIUK
SUMMER'S IN BED, BIG BOY.
LOOKS LIKE WE'VE GOT THE PLACE TO OURSELVES.
IF I DIDN'T KNOW BETTER...I'D SAY YOU'RE TRYING TO TAKE ADVANTAGE OF ME.
ACTUALLY, TO BE MORE PRECISE... I'M TRYING TO GET YOU TO TAKE ADVANTAGE OF ME.
ONCE THE CHEMO STARTS... THIS PLAYGROUND WILL BE CLOSED FOR REPAIRS.
HMMMM... WHO CAN RESIST A SIREN SONG LIKE THAT?
6-25

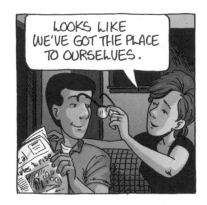

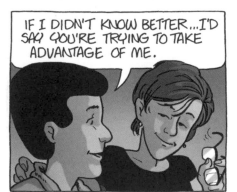

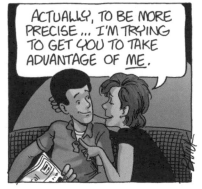

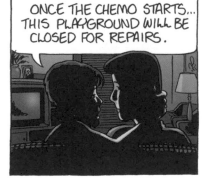

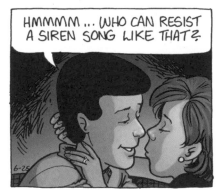

HEY, HOLLY...
I REALLY APPRECIATE YOUR TAKING LISA TO HER FIRST CHEMO SESSION.

BATIUK

NO PROBLEM...
I'VE BEEN THERE.

HOW'S LISA DOING?

6-26

SHE'S ATTACKING THIS LIKE SHE WOULD ONE OF HER LEGAL CASES.

HER CANCER DOESN'T KNOW HOW MUCH TROUBLE IT'S IN.

HOW ARE YOU DOING?

I'M DOING.

I ALWAYS GOT A LITTLE SWEATY AND NERVOUS BEFORE CHEMO.

MMM...
THAT BRINGS BACK SOME NOT SO FOND MEMORIES.

BUT FOR SUMMER'S SAKE...

I'M READY TO DEAL WITH ALL THE BAT GUANO IN THE BATCAVE.

BATIUK

6-27

97

AMAZING ... IT'S BEEN MORE THAN FIVE YEARS BUT I STILL REMEMBER WHERE TO PARK ...

6-28

WHAT FLOOR TO GO TO AND WHERE TO SIGN IN FOR THE CHEMO.

THE ONLY THING I'D FORGOTTEN WAS HOW MUCH I HATE THIS FLOOR.

DITTO.

LOOKING AT OUR RECORDS...

IT APPEARS YOU'VE GAINED A FEW POUNDS SINCE THE LAST TIME YOU WERE HERE.

IT'S JUST ONE HUMILIATION AFTER ANOTHER.

6-29

AND LOOK ... YOUR BLOOD PRESSURE'S GOING UP TOO.

SO... ARE YOU FEELING UP TO STARTING YOUR CHEMO?
MY MEDI-PORT IS STILL A LITTLE SENSITIVE, BUT OTHER THAN THAT...
I WANT YOU TO HIT ME WITH EVERYTHING YOU'VE GOT, INCLUDING THE KITCHEN SINK.
I'LL MAKE SURE TO WRITE KITCHEN SINK ON THE ORDER.
6-30

WE'RE TREATING SO MANY CANCER PATIENTS THESE DAYS THAT WE'RE A LITTLE CRAMPED FOR SPACE.
I CAN PUT YOU IN ONE OF THE SMALLER ROOMS WITH ANOTHER PATIENT...
OR, IF YOU PREFER, ROOM FOUR, THE PARTY ROOM...
4
7-1

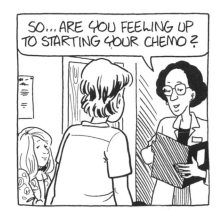

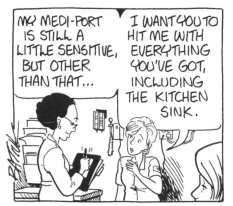

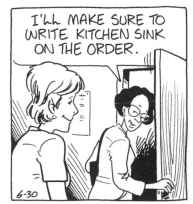

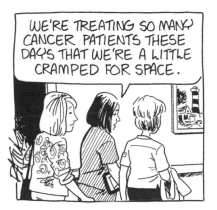

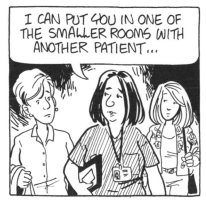

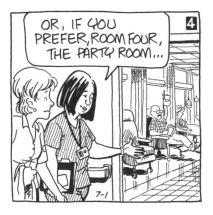

Funky Winkerbean
by Tom Batiuk

ONE WORD... CRYOGENICS.

EXCUSE ME?

CRYOGENICS.

I'M GOING TO HAVE MYSELF FROZEN JUST LIKE TED WILLIAMS.

CRYOGENICS IS HOW YOU BEAT THIS CANCER THING.

YOU HAVE YOURSELF TURNED INTO A CORPSICLE SO YOU CAN BE THAWED OUT WHEN THEY FIND A CURE.

'COURSE, NOT EVERYONE IS A CANDIDATE LIKE ME AND THE 'SPLENDID SPLINTER.' YOU'VE GOT TO BE IN TIP-TOP SHAPE OR THERE'S REALLY NO POINT TO IT.

MANY ARE CULLED...BUT FEW ARE FROZEN.

7-2

WHAT ARE YOU IN FOR?
HOW LONG HAVE YOU GOT?
CONVICTS?
REALLY?
YEAH... THAT'S WHAT SITTING AROUND TALKING WITH OTHER CHEMO PATIENTS FEELS LIKE SOMETIMES.

YOU WERE ALMOST SEVEN YEARS CANCER FREE WHEN IT RETURNED?
UH-HUH... IT CAN HAPPEN IN A SMALL PERCENTAGE OF THE CASES.
SO YOU WON THE LOTTERY.
APPARENTLY.
THE PRIZES STINK YOU KNOW...
SO I'VE HEARD.

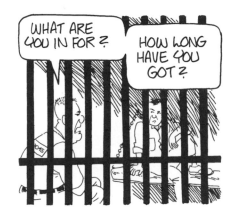

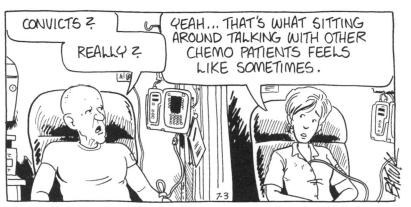

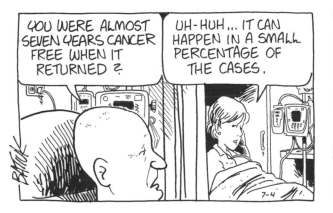

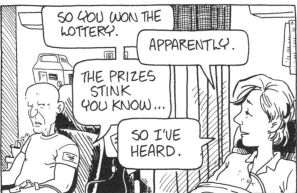

I'M JUST GLAD THAT HE'S WAS WITH ME WHEN WE MET WITH THE ONCOLOGIST.

WHENEVER I GET BAD NEWS LIKE THAT...

I'M LIKE ONE OF THOSE CHARACTERS IN A PEANUTS SPECIAL WHEN THE TEACHER IS TALKING.

ALL I HEAR IS WAH WAH WAH WAH WAH !

7-5

THE CLINICAL TRIAL IS ONLY A PHASE ONE STUDY...

SO IT'S JUST DETERMINING DOSE AND LENGTH OF TIME.

IT'S A VASCULAR DISRUPTING AGENT...

KILLS IT RIGHT IN THE BLOODSTREAM.

WITHIN A YEAR IT'S GOING TO REVOLUTIONIZE THINGS.

HOW CAN YOU SEE IF YOU'RE ELIGIBLE FOR THE TRIALS?

CANCER CERTAINLY CHANGES THE WAY YOU GOSSIP.

7-6

© 2006 Batom, Inc. Distributed by North America Syndicate Inc. All Rights Reserved.

THANKS AGAIN FOR COMING WITH ME, HOLLY.
2
IF THERE'S ONE THING I HATE ...
IT'S TRYING TO FIND YOUR CAR IN A PARKING GARAGE ON A CHEMO BRAIN.
EXIT
2

THEY GAVE HER A LOADING DOSE TO START THINGS OFF...
SO SHE MAY BE A LITTLE MOODY FOR AWHILE.
WILL WE BE ABLE TO NOTICE A DIFFERENCE ?
I HEARD THAT !

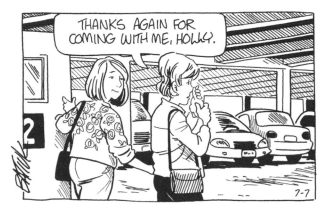

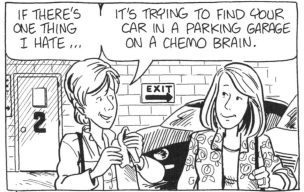

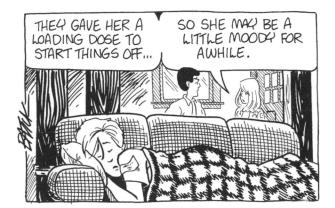

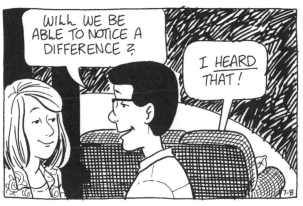

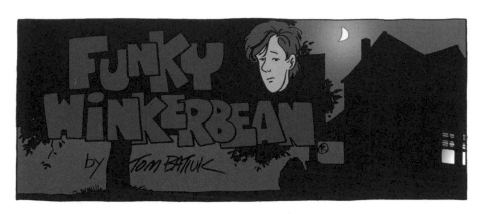

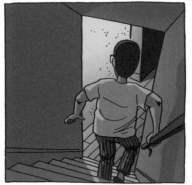

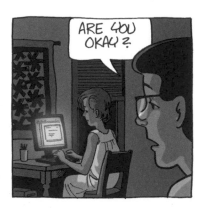

FUNKY WINKERBEAN
by TOM BATIUK
ARE YOU OKAY?
I COULDN'T SLEEP BECAUSE OF THE CHEMO ... SO I THOUGHT I'D PUT THE TIME TO GOOD USE BY CHECKING TO SEE IF THERE WERE ANY NEW DRUG TRIALS THAT I MIGHT BE A CANDIDATE FOR.
WHEN YOU'RE FIRST DIAGNOSED, IT'S LIKE JUMPING INTO A POOL...
YOU JUST SINK LIKE AN ANVIL RIGHT TO THE BOTTOM.
AND THEN GRADUALLY, LITTLE BY LITTLE, YOU START TO WORK YOUR WAY BACK UP.

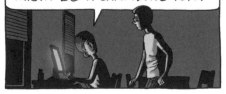

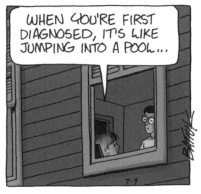

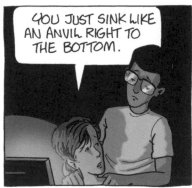

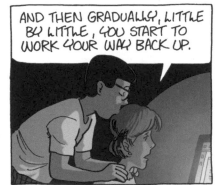

FUNKY WINKERBEAN
by TOM BATIUK
SO BEN: LE ANGOSCIE TUE NON LE VUOI DIR...
HOLLY IS HAVING A PRETTY HARD TIME DEALING WITH THE FACT THAT LISA'S CANCER HAS COME BACK.
AND I'M NOT DOING SO HOT MYSELF.
ALCOHOL WAS WHERE I USED TO RUN AND HIDE FROM LIFE.
I'LL TELL YOU WHERE I RUN AND HIDE NOW... THE SECOND ACT OF LA BOHÈME.
IT'S CHRISTMAS EVE, AND MIMI, RODOLFO AND THEIR FRIENDS ARE CELEBRATING OUTSIDE THE CAFÉ MOMUS.
IF I COULD CHOOSE A PLACE TO LIVE, IT WOULD BE THERE.
UNFORTUNATELY, JUST AS IN LIFE...
THERE'S AN ACT FOUR.

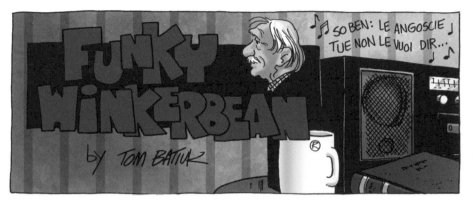

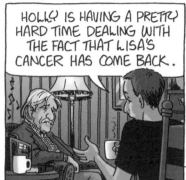

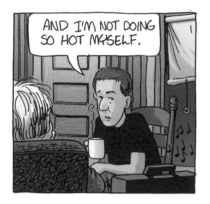

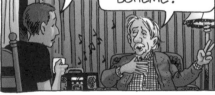

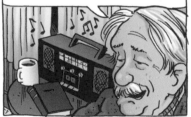

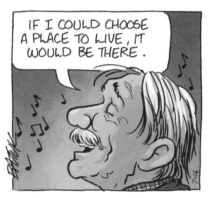

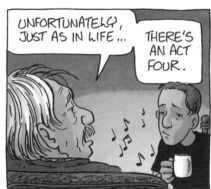

FUNKY WINKERBEAN
by TOM BATIUK
MONTONI'S
LISA MOORE
ATTORNEY AT LAW
UPSTAIRS
BATIUK
7-23

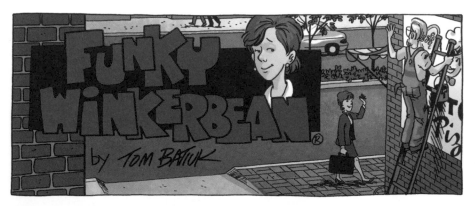

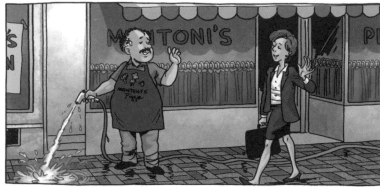

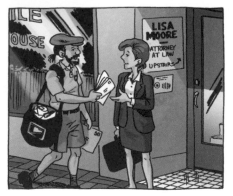

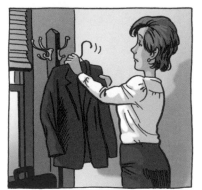

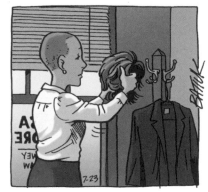

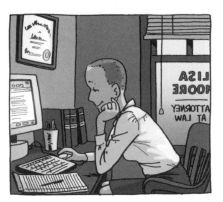

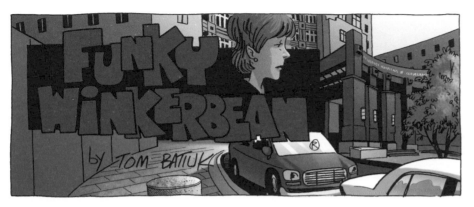

Funky Winkerbean

by Tom Batiuk

THERE'S THIS VACATION THAT WE'VE BEEN PLANNING FOR ABOUT A YEAR NOW, SO I'D LIKE TO TAKE A BREAK BEFORE MY NEXT ROUND OF CHEMO.

NORMALLY, I'D HAVE NO OBJECTION... BUT YOUR WHITE AND RED CELL COUNTS ARE BOTH PRETTY LOW.

I'LL TELL YOU WHAT, I CAN GIVE YOU SOME SHOTS TO TAKE WITH YOU THAT WILL HELP THE BONE MARROW RESUPPLY THE BODY WITH RED AND WHITE CELLS...

BUT YOU'LL NEED TO HAVE THEM INJECTED JUST UNDER THE SKIN OF YOUR STOMACH...

8-6

DO YOU THINK YOUR HUSBAND CAN DO THAT?

OH, SURE.

HE'LL BE ABLE TO GET EVEN FOR ALL THE YEARS I'VE NEEDLED HIM.

WE REALLY APPRECIATE YOU GUYS TAKING CARE OF SUMMER WHILE WE'RE ON VACATION.
HEY... NO PROBLEM.
HOW ARE YOU FEELING?
I'M THE HEALTHIEST PERSON WITH CANCER THAT I KNOW.
LIKE YOUR WIG BY THE WAY.
THANKS.
8-7

SO HOW ARE YOU DOING?
I'M OKAY... BUT CANCER CHANGES EVERYTHING.
EVERY TIME I HUG LISA...
IT'S LIKE I'M TRYING TO HOLD ONTO OUR DREAMS.
8-8

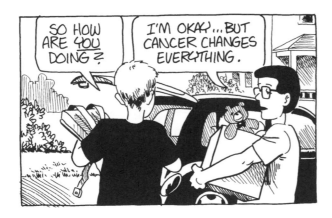

ARE YOU SURE GOING ON THIS VACATION IS A GOOD IDEA?
I'LL TAKE MY SHOTS AND I'LL BE FINE... DON'T WORRY.
8-9
BESIDES, I'VE ALWAYS WANTED TO SEE THE GRAND CANYON...
SO I THOUGHT WE'D BETTER SEE IT BEFORE...
BATIUK
BEFORE THE SUMMER'S OVER...

© 2006 Batom, Inc. Distributed by North America Syndicate Inc. All Rights Reserved
WOW! IS THIS EVER HOT!
WELCOME TO ARIDZONA!
TICKET
CHECK I
BAGGA
CLAIN
NOTICE
BATIUK
8-10

WHY DID THE INDIANS LIVE IN RUINS?

LET'S GO... I DON'T NEED TO BE REMINDED THAT SCHOOL STARTS IN A FEW WEEKS.

© 2006 Batom, Inc. Distributed by North America Syndicate Inc. All Rights Reserved.

I'M GLAD WE COULD VISIT TLAQUEPAQUE WHILE WE WERE IN SEDONA.

8-12

I WONDER WHAT TLAQUEPAQUE MEANS?

I THINK IT'S INDIAN FOR 'LET THE BUYER BEWARE'.

FUNKY WINKERBEAN
by TOM BATIUK
CAN YOU IMAGINE TRYING TO HIKE THIS TRAIL IN TENNIS SHOES ?
NO... YOU CALLED IT.
IT'S A GOOD THING I MADE US GET SOME GOOD HIKING SHOES FOR THE TRAILS IN THE CANYON...
GREAT IDEA.
AND THAT I HAD US BREAK THEM IN BEFORE WE LEFT.
ABSOLUTELY.
8-13
BATIUK
YOU'RE LUCKY I'M NOT THE KIND TO SAY 'I TOLD YOU SO.'
I KNOW... LUCKY ME...

WHAT DO YOU SAY WE STOP FOR A SEC AND CATCH OUR BREATH?
8-14

IS THAT CANADA ON THE OTHER SIDE?
TIME TO GO.
REMINDING YOU OF SCHOOL AGAIN?
YEP.
8-15

DRY HEAT OR NOT... THIS IS HOT!
NAVAHO
MOTEL
VACANCY
I KNOW... I'M SO HOT...
8-16
THAT MY HOT FLASHES FROM THE CHEMO ARE COOLING ME OFF.
BATIUK
WESTVIEW

YOU KNOW... IT WOULD BE NICE TO GET BACK TO THE DAYS WHEN A 'SHOT'...
BATIUK
8-17
WAS JUST A DRINKING TERM.

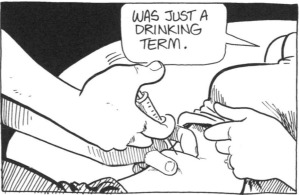

OH, DON'T BE SUCH A POOP...
OPEN
OPEN DAILY
YOU HAD A GOOD TIME HIKING THE GRAND CANYON AND ZION CANYON WILL BE JUST AS MUCH FUN.
OKAY... BUT JUST FOR GRINS, LET'S ASK THEM IF THEY HAVE ANY HANDICAPPED ACCESS HIKING TRAILS.
8-18

ARE YOU COMING?
I'D LIKE TO...
BUT SOMEONE HAS TO STAY BEHIND TO TAKE THE PICTURES.
8-19

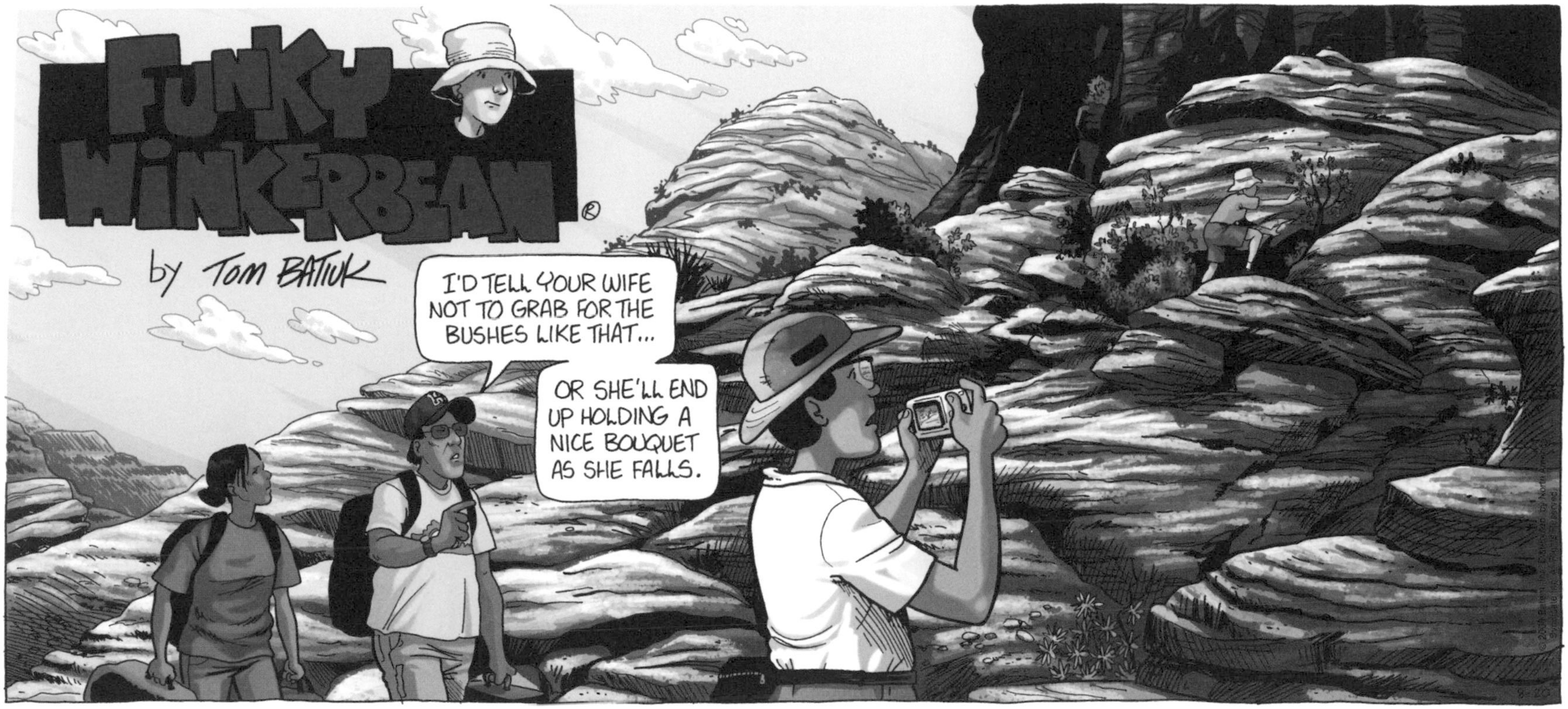
FUNKY WINKERBEAN®
by TOM BATIUK
I'D TELL YOUR WIFE NOT TO GRAB FOR THE BUSHES LIKE THAT...
OR SHE'LL END UP HOLDING A NICE BOUQUET AS SHE FALLS.

LISA, THIS IS DAVID AND HIS DAUGHTER NATANE.

HE WAS THE ONE WHO HAD ME WARN YOU ABOUT GRABBING THE BUSHES...

8-21

YOU SHOULD ALSO TEST EACH HAND HOLD TO MAKE SURE THE ROCK ISN'T LOOSE...

YOU DON'T WANT TO END UP WITH A 'SOUVENIR HOLD'.

MY DAUGHTER IS GRADUATING FROM COMMUNITY COLLEGE THIS SUMMER AND WE CAME UP HERE TO TAKE SOME GRADUATION PICTURES.

I'D APPRECIATE IT IF YOU WOULDN'T MENTION THE WORD 'SCHOOL' AROUND MY HUSBAND.

8-22

THAT'S VERY PRETTY.
THANK YOU... MY GRANDMOTHER MADE IT FOR ME FOR GRADUATION.
8-23
WHAT WAS THAT?
NOTHING, SWEETIE.

DAD... YOU'RE STILL MISSING THE HAIR BY MY EARS!
WHAT HAIR?
THESE WISPS.
WHAT WISPS?
8-24
THAT'S IT!
GIVE ME THE BRUSH!

I DON'T BELIEVE IT... I FORGOT MY CAMERA.
WAS IT DIGITAL?
YEAH...
PROBLEM SOLVED.
YOU CAN USE MINE AND I'LL BURN YOU A CD WHEN I GET HOME.
GREAT... THEN I CAN JUST UPLOAD IT TO MY COMPUTER.
8-25

8-26

FUNKY WINKERBEAN
by TOM BATIUK
THANK YOU VERY MUCH FOR YOUR CAMERA.
YOU BET... AND I'LL SEND THE PICTURES AS SOON AS WE GET HOME.
8-27
LIVE WITH HOPE.
BATIUK

Three months later

FUNKY WINKERBEAN
by TOM BATIUK
WESTVIEW BAND
THANKS FOR YOUR ORDER, MRS. MOORE.
YOUR BAND FRUITCAKE WILL BE DELIVERED IN ABOUT A WEEK.
DO YOU NEED A PAIN PILL?
NO THANKS... DIFFERENT KIND OF PAIN.
SEEING DARIN FAIRGOOD REMINDED ME THAT THE BABY I GAVE UP WOULD BE A SENIOR IN HIGH SCHOOL RIGHT NOW.
BATIUK
12-3.
WHAT DO YOU SAY WE DO SOMETHING TO BRIGHTEN YOUR MOOD?
MOMMEEE... LOOK AT ME.
THANKS... BUT IT'S ALREADY BEEN TAKEN CARE OF.

DON'T WORRY,... IT'S JUST ME... I ALWAYS THINK OF...

THE BABY, I KNOW... ON HIS BIRTHDAY...

12-4

WHAT DO YOU SAY WE DROP SUMMER OFF AT YOUR FOLKS AND STOP BY CRAZY AND DONNA'S ANNIVERSARY PARTY AT MONTONI'S?

I DO DECLARE...YOU CERTAINLY KNOW HOW TO TURN A GAL'S HEAD.

I HOPE MY FOLKS DON'T FEEL BAD...

THEY ALWAYS USED TO BRING ME HERE TO MONTONI'S FOR MY BIRTHDAY.

PRIVATE PARTY

MAYBE IT'S TIME FOR A NEW TRADITION.

JEEZ... GET A ROOM, YOU TWO.

COULD YOU FIND ME SOMETHING IN THE NON-SMOOCHING SECTION?

SORRY... THERE'S A PRIVATE PARTY IN THERE.

12-5

HOW'S LISA DOING?
HER LAST SCAN SHOWED THAT HER CANCER HAD PROGRESSED SOME.
SORRY...
YEAH... BUT WE'RE TRYING TO GET HER ACCEPTED FOR A NEW CLINICAL TRIAL.
12-6
HOW IS ALL OF THIS NOT MAKING YOU TOTALLY NUTS!?
WE HAVE A TERM FOR IT AT OUR HOUSE...
WE CALL IT TUESDAY.

HERE WE ARE AT OUR THIRD ANNIVERSARY ALREADY...
AND THEY SAID IT WOULDN'T LAST...
NOT ONLY THAT, BUT MY SIDEKICK AND I WOULD LIKE TO ANNOUNCE THAT A NEW MEMBER WILL BE JOINING OUR MERRY LITTLE BAND IN ABOUT EIGHT MONTHS, GIVE OR TAKE.
I DON'T BELIEVE IT.
WESTVIEW COACH
12-7

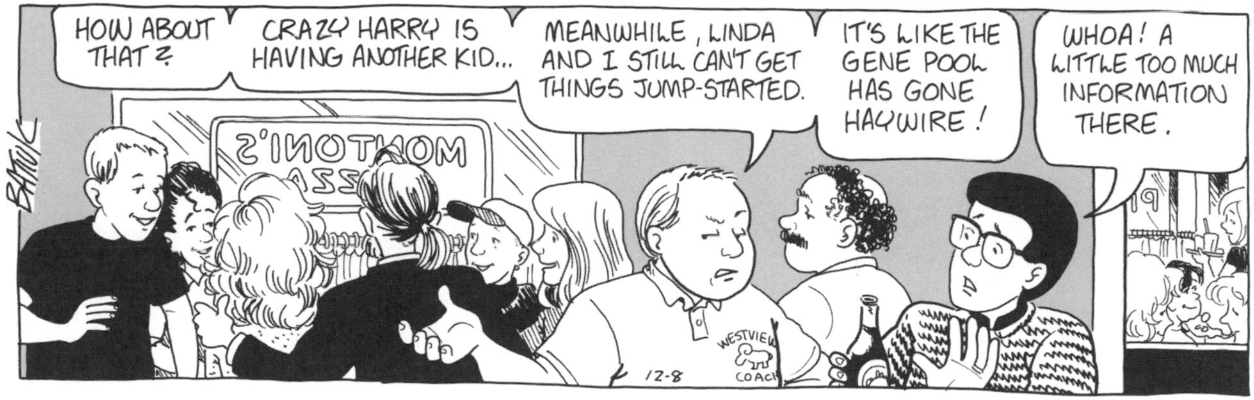
HOW ABOUT THAT?
CRAZY HARRY IS HAVING ANOTHER KID...
MEANWHILE, LINDA AND I STILL CAN'T GET THINGS JUMP-STARTED.
IT'S LIKE THE GENE POOL HAS GONE HAYWIRE!
WHOA! A LITTLE TOO MUCH INFORMATION THERE.
MONTONI'S PIZZA
WESTVIEW COACH
12-8

FUNKY WINKERBEAN
by TOM BATIUK

IT'S TIME TO TOAST THE NEW YEAR WITH SOME FINE SPARKLING GRAPE JUICE.

WHAT YEAR IS THE GRAPE JUICE?

THIS YEAR I HOPE.

HERE'S TO 2007... AND A SUCCESSFUL CLINICAL TRIAL.

UH, NOT QUITE YET...

OH, RIGHT...

HAPPY NEW YEAR!

IT'S LOOKING GOOD FOR A SNOW DAY?...

WE'VE GOT TWO INCHES OF SNOW SO FAR.

SO WE'RE STAYING UP TO WATCH LETTERMAN TONIGHT?

YOU BET!

1-5

WHAT'S THAT?

IT'S MY TEACHERS PHONE TREE.

1-6

IT'S THE TEACHERS I HAVE TO CALL IN CASE THERE'S A SNOW DAY.

THIS WAY I CAN CALL THEM RIGHT FROM BED AND THEN ROLL OVER AND GO RIGHT BACK TO SLEEP.

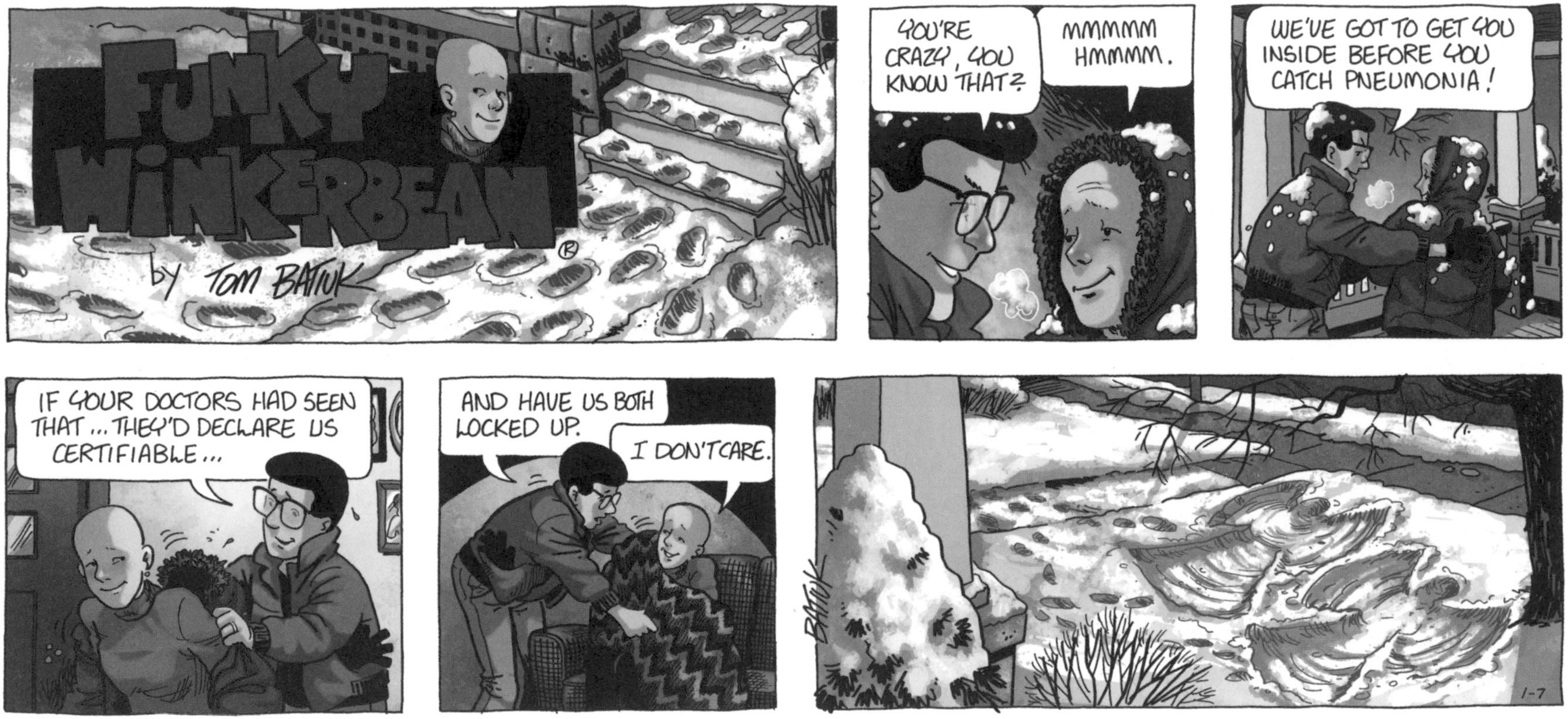
FUNKY WINKERBEAN
by TOM BATIUK
YOU'RE CRAZY, YOU KNOW THAT?
MMMMM HMMMM.
WE'VE GOT TO GET YOU INSIDE BEFORE YOU CATCH PNEUMONIA!
IF YOUR DOCTORS HAD SEEN THAT... THEY'D DECLARE US CERTIFIABLE...
AND HAVE US BOTH LOCKED UP.
I DON'T CARE.
BATIUK
1-7

Three weeks later

HEY, WHAT'S UP?

HEY, FUNKY.

I'M JUST TRYING TO CATCH UP ON SOME CHORES THAT I'VE LET SLIDE DURING LISA'S CHEMO TREATMENTS.

SUCH AS...?

SUCH AS FINALLY GETTING AROUND TO BRINGING THE HOSE IN.

1-22

LISA SEES HER ONCOLOGIST ON THURSDAY AND WILL HAVE ANOTHER SCAN.

1-23

I'M ALWAYS ON PINS AND NEEDLES UNTIL THE REPORTS ARE BACK.

I KNOW... I'M THE SAME WAY.

NOBODY SAID IT WOULD BE EASY.

AND NOBODY SAID IT WOULD HURT THIS MUCH EITHER.

IT'S FUNNY...BACK IN HIGH SCHOOL I HATED BEING YOUNG...

AND NOW I'M SCARED OF BEING OLD.

1-24

YEAH...THE HITS JUST KEEP ON COMING, DON'T THEY?

NOT ONLY IS BECKY BACK AT WORK...BUT I HEAR SHE'S GOING TO BE THE NEW BAND DIRECTOR AT THE HIGH SCHOOL.

1-25

WOW...A NEW BABY... A NEW JOB...A HUSBAND FIGHTING IN IRAQ...

BUCKLE UP

AND ALL I CAN THINK ABOUT IS MY CANCER.

YOU LOOK GOOD... YOU SOUND GOOD... AND YOUR COUNTS ARE RIGHT WHERE YOU SHOULD BE...
BUT LET'S WAIT AND SEE WHAT THE REPORTS FROM THE SCAN HAVE TO SAY...
OSPITAL
I DON'T WANT TO GIVE YOU ANY FALSE HOPE.
THAT'S OKAY... SOMETIMES EVEN FALSE HOPE HELPS.
BATIUK
1-26

WE GOT A LETTER FROM DENNIS, THE NAVAHO INDIAN WE MET WHEN WE WERE IN THE SOUTHWEST.
BATIUK
HE SENT US A COPY OF HIS DAUGHTER'S GRADUATION PICTURE.
1-27
Live with hope.

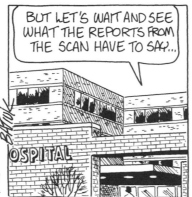

ARE THE RESULTS FROM MY SCAN IN ?
OSPITAL
YES, I HAVE THEM RIGHT HERE AND I'M NOT QUITE SURE HOW TO PUT THIS...
1-29
HOW ARE YOU AT HANDLING GOOD NEWS ?
BATIUK

IT LOOKS LIKE YOUR SCANS ARE CLEAR...
YOU APPEAR TO BE A COMPLETE RESPONDER.
I DON'T KNOW WHAT TO SAY...
BATIUK
1-30
I'D SAY YOU'RE IN REMISSION.

WOW! I'M CONFUSED.

TELL ME WHAT JUST HAPPENED IN THE DOCTOR'S OFFICE TODAY.

I THINK THE GOVERNOR CALLED AND SAID...

'NOT YET.'

1-31

I STILL CAN'T BELIEVE IT.

NEITHER CAN I ...

I WAS SO BRACED FOR BAD NEWS... THAT I'M HAVING TROUBLE PROCESSING THE GOOD NEWS.

2-1

MAYBE FOR THE FIRST TIME IN MONTHS...

I CAN LIE IN BED LISTENING TO MY HEART BEAT, AND NOT HAVE IT SOUND LIKE A TICKING BOMB.

2-2
BATIUK

IT LOOKS LIKE THE NEWS OF LISA'S REMISSION HAS DONE WONDERS.
BATIUK
2-3
THE CARE LINES ARE GONE AND THERE'S JUST THIS POSITIVE GLOW.
YEAH, SHE'S ON CLOUD NINE.
I WAS TALKING ABOUT YOU.

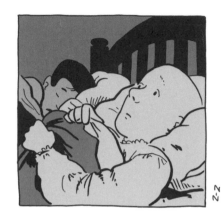

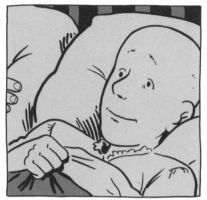

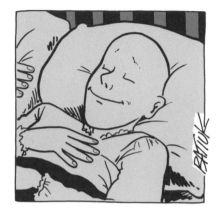

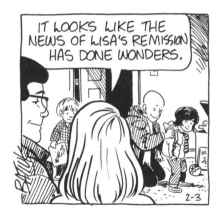

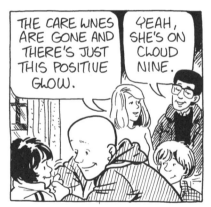

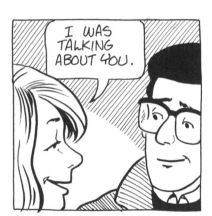

One month later

YOU'RE LOOKING GREAT, LISA ... I LIKE YOUR HAIR.

THANKS, HOLLY ... EVERYONE SAYS THAT ...

BUT I DON'T SEE ANYONE RUSHING OUT TO GET THEIR HAIR CUT LIKE THIS.

2-26

I'VE STILL GOT SOME NEUROPATHY IN MY FEET FROM THE CHEMO ... BUT, YOU KNOW, MY HAIR'S COMING BACK AND MY ENERGY LEVEL IS PICKING UP ...

2-27

OH, REALLY ... ?

YEAH ... EVEN ...

I FELT LIKE I WAS EIGHTEEN AGAIN ...

NERVOUS, UNSURE AND AWKWARD.

133

I'VE JUST SORT OF BEEN SPENDING MY TIME TAKING IT EASY...

READING, ENJOYING SUMMER... JUST ENJOYING BEING HERE REALLY.

THEY SAY THAT HAVING CANCER CAN GIVE MEANING TO LIFE.

WELL, JUST BETWEEN YOU, ME AND THE MICROWAVE...

I THINK I'D RATHER FIND MEANING IN HAPPIER WAYS, THANK YOU VERY MUCH.

2-28

YOU KNOW, HOLLY, IT'S NICE TO HAVE A FELLOW CANCER CLUB MEMBER TO TALK SHOP WITH.

3-1

MOST OF THE TIME IT'S THE ELEPHANT IN THE ROOM THAT NO ONE WANTS TO TALK ABOUT.

IT'S ALWAYS HARD DEALING WITH CIVILIANS...

THEY NEVER KNOW WHAT TO SAY.

WHEN ALL THEY HAVE TO REALLY SAY IS THAT.

SO YOU'RE GOING TO SEE AN ACUPUNCTURIST FOR THE PAIN IN YOUR FEET FROM THE CHEMO

YEAH, THEY WORK OUT OF THIS PAIN MANAGEMENT CLINIC IN PAINESVILLE.

YOU'RE SEEING SOMEONE FOR PAIN MANAGEMENT IN PAINESVILLE?

TOO WEIRD.

WELCOME TO MY WORLD.

3-2

I'VE ALSO STARTED DOING SOME TAI CHI TO HELP KEEP MY ANXIETIES IN CHECK AND TO LOWER MY STRESS LEVELS.

3-3

SMART MOVE...THE BIGGEST THING WE HAVE TO FEAR IS FEAR ITSELF.

THAT AND THE CANCER.

EXACTLY.

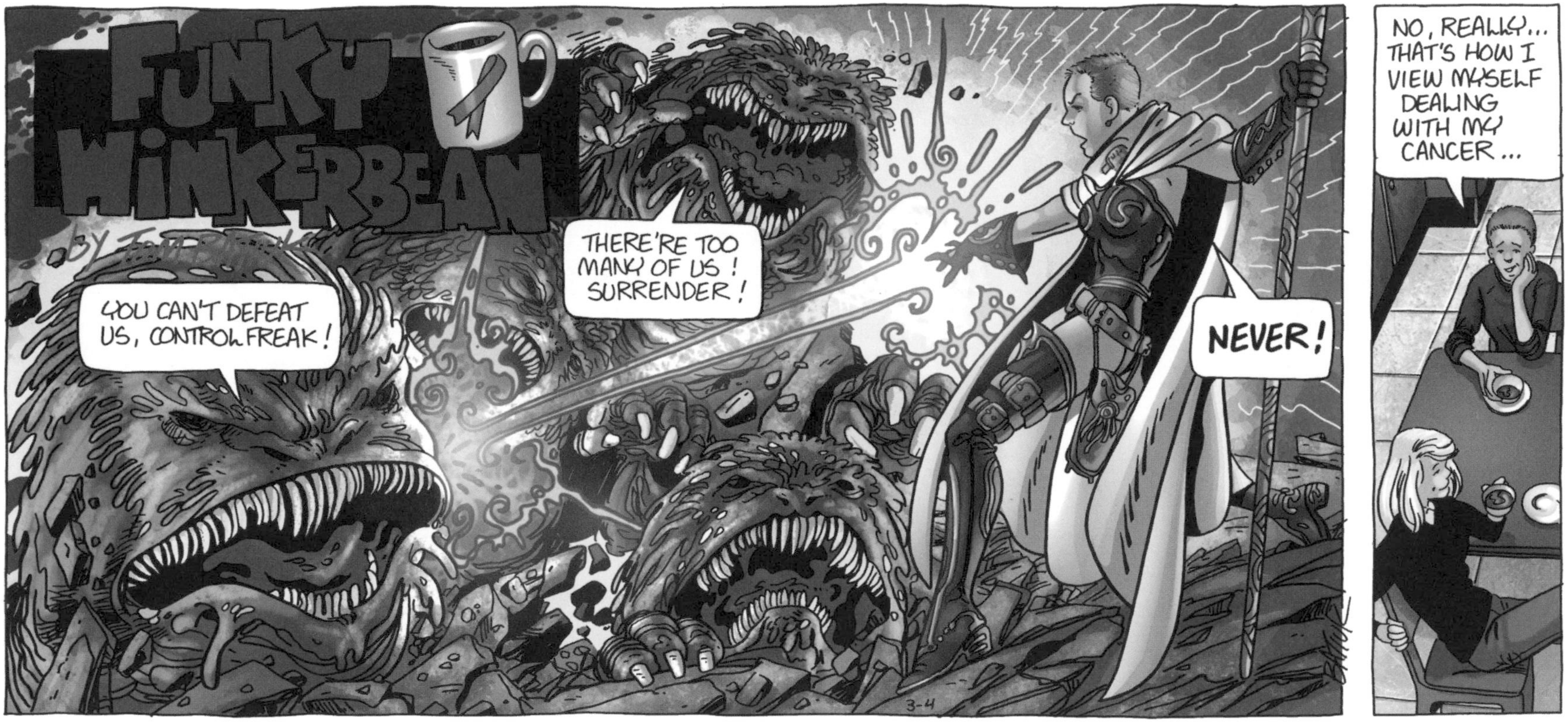
FUNKY WINKERBEAN
YOU CAN'T DEFEAT US, CONTROL FREAK!
THERE'RE TOO MANY OF US! SURRENDER!
NEVER!
3-4
NO, REALLY... THAT'S HOW I VIEW MYSELF DEALING WITH MY CANCER...

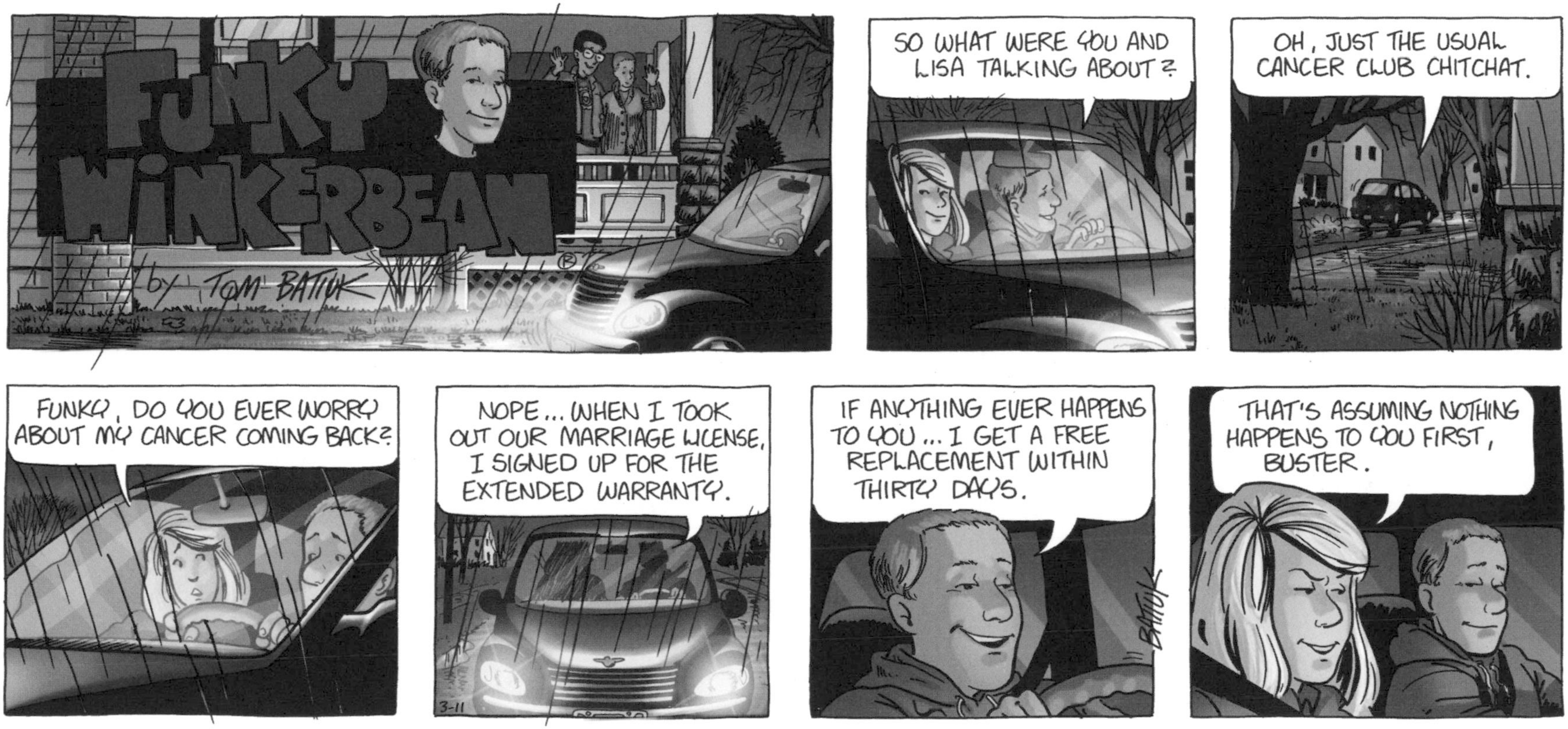
FUNKY WINKERBEAN
by TOM BATIUK
SO WHAT WERE YOU AND LISA TALKING ABOUT?
OH, JUST THE USUAL CANCER CLUB CHITCHAT.
FUNKY, DO YOU EVER WORRY ABOUT MY CANCER COMING BACK?
NOPE... WHEN I TOOK OUT OUR MARRIAGE LICENSE, I SIGNED UP FOR THE EXTENDED WARRANTY.
3-11
IF ANYTHING EVER HAPPENS TO YOU... I GET A FREE REPLACEMENT WITHIN THIRTY DAYS.
BATIUK
THAT'S ASSUMING NOTHING HAPPENS TO YOU FIRST, BUSTER.

I'LL LET YOU OFF THIS TIME... BUT SAY ONE WORD ABOUT IT...
AND I'LL COME BACK AND FINISH THE JOB!! UNDERSTAND ME!?
3-26
YEAH, SURE... IT WON'T LEAVE THIS ROOM. WHAT'S UP?

LISTEN... I'VE GOT NEWS FOR YOU...
REALLY? SO YOU AND LINDA ARE THINKING ABOUT ADOPTING?
WELL... YOU'RE HALF RIGHT.
3-27

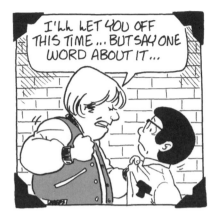

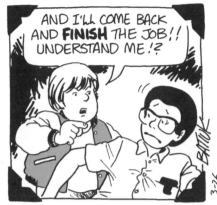

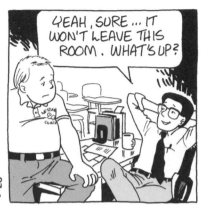

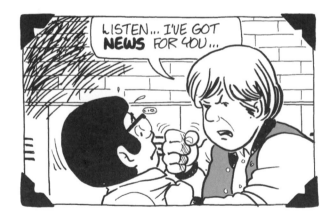

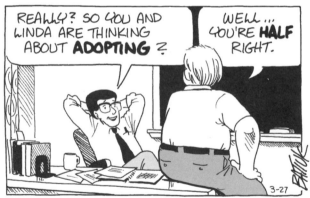

IT'S NOT AN EASY DECISION...
BUT AT LEAST THIS WAY WE'LL BOTH HAVE A CHANCE TO GROW UP.
3-28
SO THAT'S WHY SHE DROPPED OUT OF...
LISA HAD A BABY OUR SENIOR YEAR AND GAVE IT UP FOR ADOPTION...
EXACTLY.
AND SHE'S ALWAYS BEEN GRATEFUL TO WHOEVER IT WAS WHO ADOPTED THAT BABY.
BATIUK

WILL BULL BUSHKA PLEASE REPORT TO THE PRINCIPAL'S OFFICE IMMEDIATELY!
BATIUK
YOU WANTED TO SEE ME, FRED?
WHS
PRINCIPAL
3-29

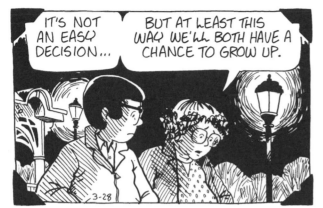

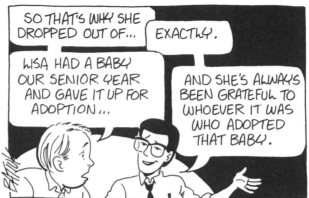

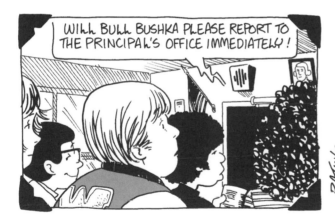

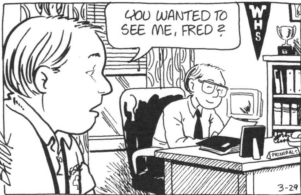

HERE, LET ME GET THE DOOR SO I CAN SAY I HELPED WITH THE DELIVERY.
AND WHEN LINDA MENTIONED THAT YOU GUYS WERE THINKING ABOUT ADOPTING TOO...
WELL, I JUST WANTED TO LET YOU KNOW THAT WE'D BE HAPPY TO ANSWER ANY QUESTIONS THAT YOU MAY HAVE.
3-30

PSSST... HOW MUCH IS TWO AND TWO?
3-31
AMAZING... IT SOUNDS LIKE FRED AND ANN ADOPTED THEIR BABY THE SAME YEAR THAT LISA GAVE HER BABY UP FOR ADOPTION.
TALK ABOUT YOUR AMAZING COINCIDENCES.
MR. FAIRGOOD
PRINCIPAL

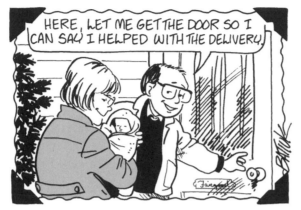

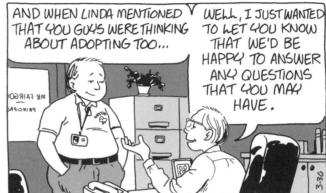

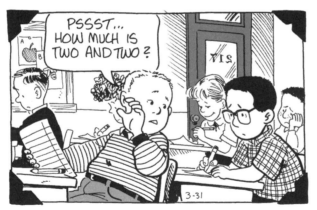

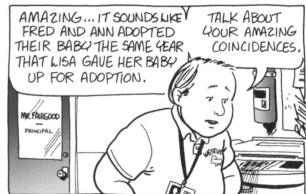

DO YOU **WANT** TO?
YEAH... BUT NOT YET, IS THAT OKAY?
'COURSE.
HEY... WHAT'S **THAT**?

OOH... FAMILY ALBUM!
AW, YOU WERE **SUCH** A CUTE **BABY**!
WOULD YOU **PLEASE** PUT THAT **BACK**?
NOT SUCH A CUTE BABY **RIGHT NOW**, THOUGH...

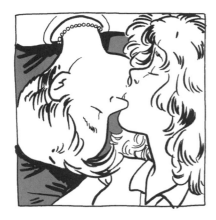

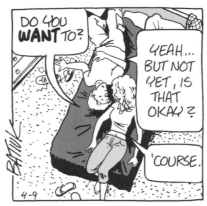

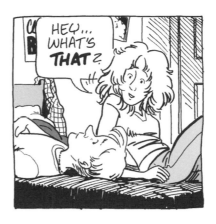

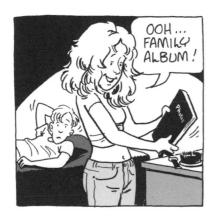

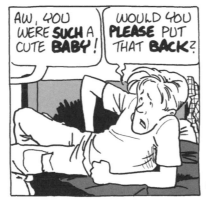

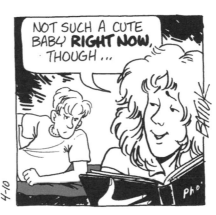

WOW... YOU REALLY DO LOOK LIKE YOUR PARENTS.
YOU SURE ABOUT THAT? 'CAUSE YOU KNOW...
4-11
I'M ADOPTED.

DARIN... I HAD NO IDEA YOU WERE ADOPTED.
IT'S NO BIG DEAL.
4-12
I WAS ADOPTED AT BIRTH, SO AS FAR AS I'M CONCERNED...
MY PARENTS ARE MY PARENTS.

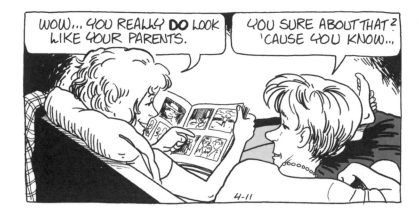

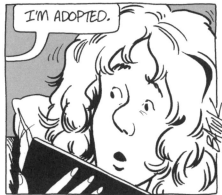

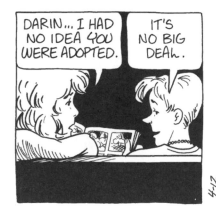

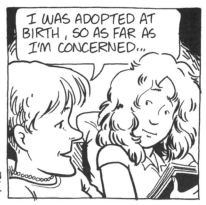

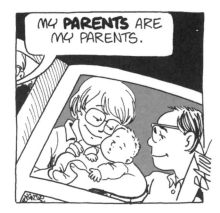

AREN'T YOU THE LEAST BIT CURIOUS WHO YOUR BIRTH PARENTS ARE?
I DUNNO... NEVER REALLY THOUGHT ABOUT IT I GUESS...
WELL...
MAYBE YOU **SHOULD** THINK ABOUT IT.

JESS... THERE'S NO **POINT** IN LOOKING UP MY BIRTH PARENTS.
I DON'T EVEN KNOW IF I LEGALLY **CAN**.

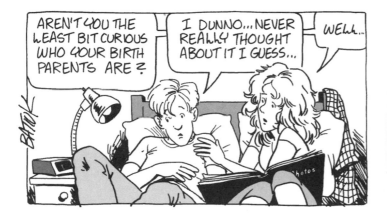

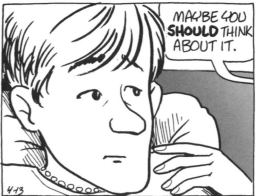

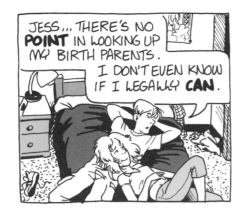

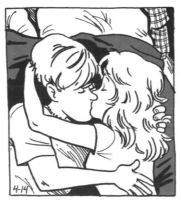

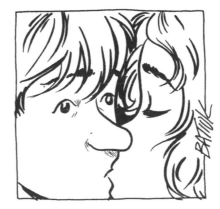

THERE YOU ARE ...
BATIUK
HEY.
HEY.
4-16
Darin

YOU STILL WANT ME TO LOOK UP MY BIRTH PARENTS ?
OHIO DEPARTMENT OF JOB AND
ADOPTIVE INFORMATION
JESS, I **TOLD** YOU I'M NOT...
JESS... ?
4-17
BATIUK
DARIN ... DID I EVER TELL YOU ABOUT MY FATHER ?

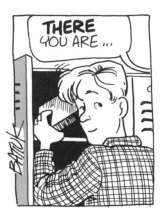

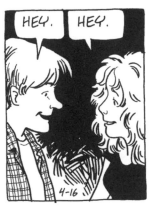

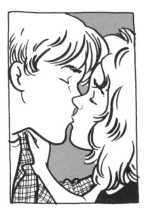

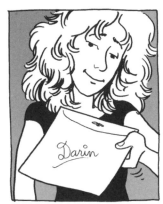

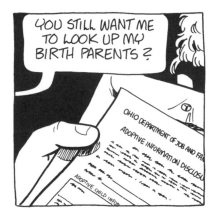

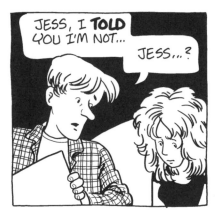

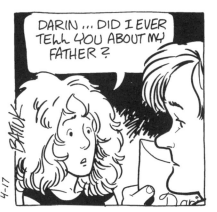

BAND ROOM
NO CIVILIANS ALLOWED!
WHS
YOUR DAD WAS JOHN DARLING, THE TALK SHOW HOST, RIGHT?
YEAH.
I KNOW HE PASSED AWAY SOME TIME AGO, BUT...
ACTUALLY, HE WAS **MURDERED**.
BATIUK
4-18

'MY DAD... HE'D FINISHED HIS LAST SHOW...'
'WHEN A CRAZY GUEST SHOT HIM AS HE LEFT THE SET.'
BLAM!
I WAS TOO YOUNG TO REMEMBER HIM.
BATIUK
4-19

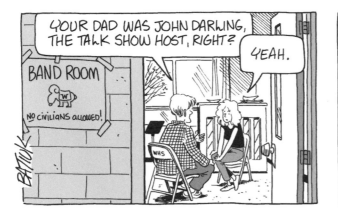

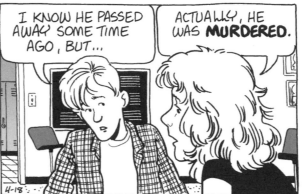

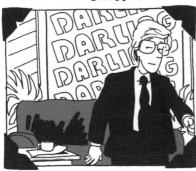

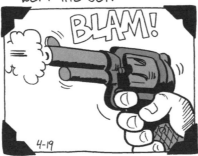

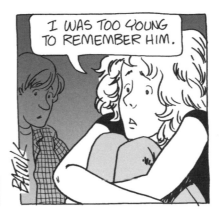

I NEVER **KNEW** MY DAD, JUST LIKE YOU NEVER KNEW YOUR **BIRTH PARENTS**.
BUT, DARIN ... IF THERE **WAS** ANY WAY I COULD SEE HIM TODAY...
4-20
I'D GIVE **ANYTHING** FOR THAT CHANCE.

LOOK, JESSE... I CAN'T PROMISE I'LL ACTUALLY **TALK** TO MY BIRTH PARENTS...
4-21
BUT I'LL LOOK 'EM UP, OKAY?

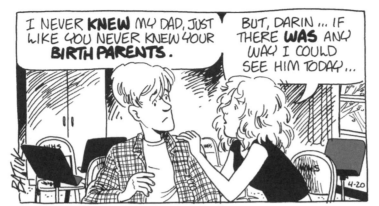

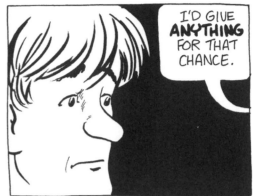

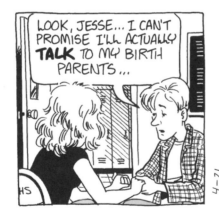

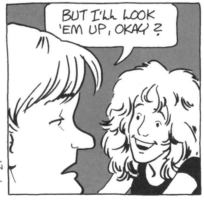

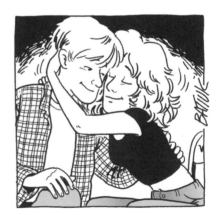

WHAT ARE WE DOING **HERE?**
MY PARENTS...
THEY DON'T KNOW THAT I'M LOOKING UP MY BIRTH PARENTS...
SO I'M GETTING A POST OFFICE BOX.
HOPEFULLY, THIS YEAR.
STAMPS · ENVELOPES · BOXES
PLEASE WAIT HERE
4-23

HERE, TAKE THE KEY.
WHAT? WHY?
YOU'RE THE ONE WHO REALLY WANTS ME TO FIND MY BIRTH PARENTS, SO...
NUH-UH.
I WANT IT FOR **YOU.**
4-24

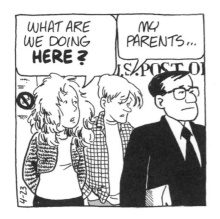

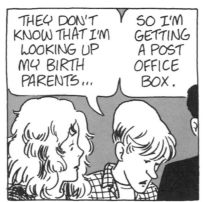

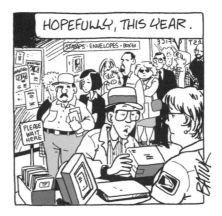

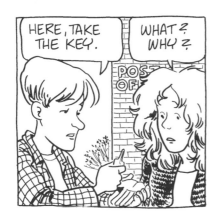

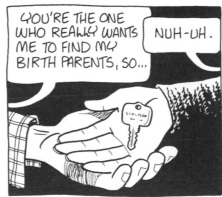

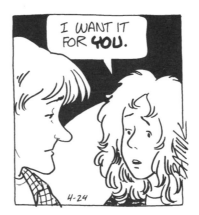

DARIN...

DON'T YOU WANT TO... YOU KNOW?

JESS... OF COURSE I WANT TO.

BUT IF YOU **REALLY** DO, THEN YOU **WOULD**.

YOU DON'T THINK I'M SEXY!

YEAH, THAT'S RIGHT... AND FRENCH FRIES HAVE BEEN PROVEN TO BE HELPFUL IN LOWERING CHOLESTEROL.

I'M SORRY, JESS... I REALLY **DO** WANT TO BE WITH YOU...
... BUT I'M NOT READY. THE TIME HAS TO BE RIGHT.
... NOW. YOU MEANT TO SAY 'RIGHT **NOW**'.
4-27

UNITED STATES
POST
OFFICE
POST OFFICE
4-28

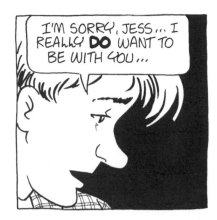

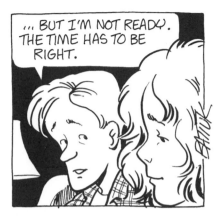

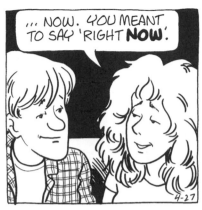

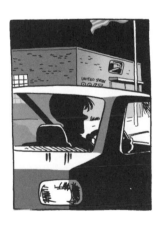

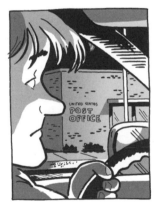

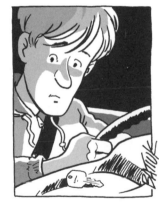

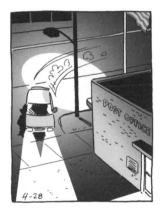

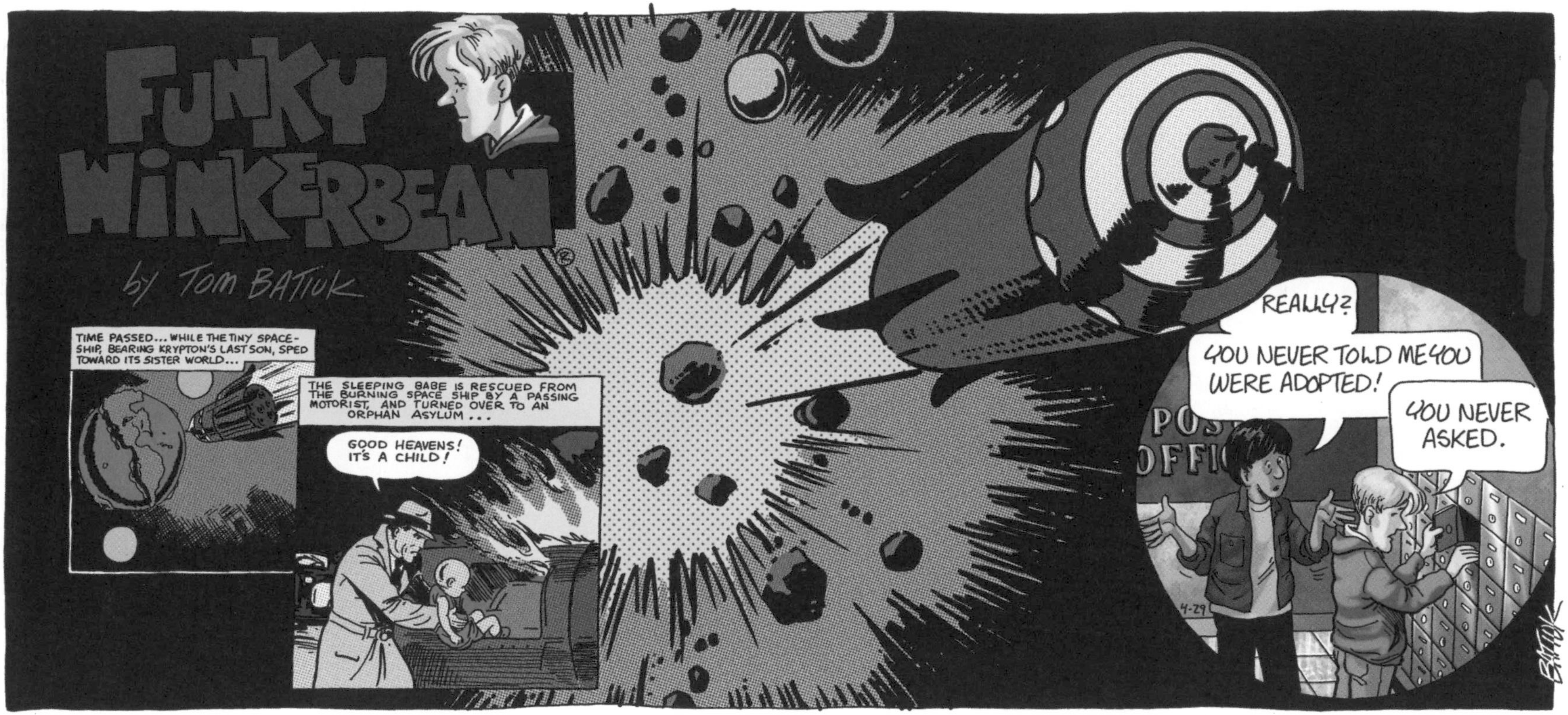
FUNKY WINKERBEAN
by TOM BATIUK
TIME PASSED... WHILE THE TINY SPACE-SHIP, BEARING KRYPTON'S LAST SON, SPED TOWARD ITS SISTER WORLD...
THE SLEEPING BABE IS RESCUED FROM THE BURNING SPACE SHIP BY A PASSING MOTORIST, AND TURNED OVER TO AN ORPHAN ASYLUM...
GOOD HEAVENS! IT'S A CHILD!
YOU NEVER TOLD ME YOU WERE ADOPTED!
REALLY?
YOU NEVER ASKED.
POST OFFIC
4-29
BATIUK

HOW HAS YOUR PAIN BEEN?
ATLAS OF ACUPUNCTURE POINTS
BETTER I THINK... SOME DAYS MORE THAN OTHERS.
THEN WE'LL TRY TO ONLY ACCESS THE POINTS THAT PROVIDE GOOD DAYS.
SOUNDS LIKE A PLAN.
BATIUK
4-30

I'VE GOT A SCAN COMING UP ON THURSDAY...
AND I'M USUALLY ON PINS AND NEEDLES BEFORE A SCAN...
SO THIS ACTUALLY FITS RIGHT IN.
AS IF I'VE NEVER HEARD THAT JOKE BEFORE.
BATIUK
5-1

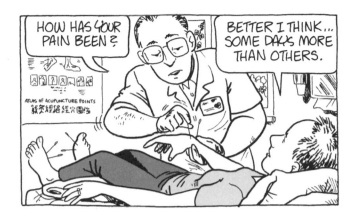

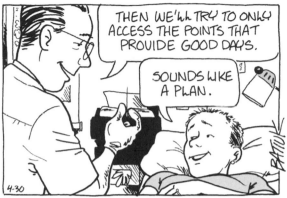

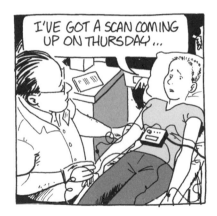

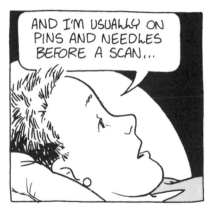

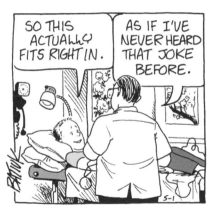

I'M GOING INTO MY OFFICE TO TRY AND GET A LITTLE WORK DONE...

AND THEN I'VE GOT MY SCAN AFTER LUNCH.

POOF! THERE GOES HALF A DAY I'LL NEVER SEE AGAIN.

5-2

BEFORE I GO AND CHANGE FOR MY SCAN... I HAVE A QUESTION ABOUT MY BILL.

ON MY LAST INVOICE, ALONG WITH THE SCAN ITSELF, I'M NOW BEING CHARGED FOR SOMETHING CALLED A FACILITY FEE.

PLEASE SIGN IN

THAT'S A SEPARATE CHARGE MADE BY THE HOSPITAL FOR THE USE OF ITS FACILITY.

I DON'T SUPPOSE THERE'S ANY CHANCE OF HAVING THE SCAN DONE IN THE PARKING LOT.

I'M AFRAID THE EQUIPMENT IS WAY TOO BIG TO...

THAT WAS A JOKE. SORT OF...

5-3

JUST RELAX...

SORRY, I'M A LITTLE NERVOUS.

ARE YOU AFRAID OF SMALL ENCLOSED SPACES?

NO... JUST SMALL ENCLOSED SPACES THAT IRRADIATE MY BODY WHILE LOOKING FOR BAD THINGS.

5-4

OUR HMO HAS DENIED THE HOSPITAL'S FACILITY FEE.

IN OTHER WORDS, THEY'LL PAY FOR THE SCAN, BUT NOT FOR THE LIGHT BULB IN THE ROOM WHERE THE SCAN TAKES PLACE.

5-5

THAT MAKES SENSE ACTUALLY...
THE LIGHT BULB'S TENDENCY TO BURN OUT WAS A PRE-EXISTING CONDITION.

DO WE HAVE LISA MOORE'S LATEST SCANS BACK YET?
YES... I JUST SAW THEM HERE SOMEWHERE.
5-7
WOULD YOU PLEASE GET LISA MOORE ON THE PHONE FOR ME?

DR. HALLETT WANTED TO SEE YOU TODAY?
5-8
YES... SHE WANTED TO GO OVER MY SCANS AND PROBABLY DIDN'T WANT TO DO IT ON THE PHONE.
OKAY...
HERE... DON'T FORGET TO TAKE YOUR PHONE WITH YOU.

THERE WAS A MIX-UP WITH SOME SCANS IN RADIOLOGY... AND APPARENTLY THE SCANS WE LOOKED AT THREE MONTHS AGO WEREN'T YOURS.
YOUR LATEST SCANS SHOW THAT THE DISEASE HAS PROGRESSED.
WE SCREWED UP... I'M SORRY.
DR. HALLETT
5-9
YOU'RE SORRY!!? THEIR INCOMPETENT BUNGLING HAS PUT MY LIFE ON THE LINE, AND ALL YOU CAN SAY IS YOU'RE SORRY!!? OOPS!!?
OKAY... WHAT DO WE DO NOW?

HEY, FAIR IS FAIR... HAND OVER YOUR PHONE AND LET'S SEE WHO'S CALLING.
BREEP! BREEP!
5-10
I NEED YOU.
I'M COMING.
DR. HALLETT
ONCOLOGIST

I WON'T KID YOU...THE FACT THAT THERE ARE NEW TUMORS IS VERY SERIOUS.

DR. HALLETT
ONCOLOGIST

5-11

THE GOOD NEWS IS THAT HAVING BEEN OFF CHEMO FOR THREE MONTHS ... YOU'RE PROBABLY ELIGIBLE NOW FOR THAT TRIAL WE TRIED TO GET YOU IN EARLIER ...

AND AGAIN...

I KNOW ... YOU'RE SORRY.

MRS. WILSON & DR. HALLETT... I HAVE SOME GOOD NEWS.

DR. HALLETT
ONCOLOGIST

5-12

FUNKY WINKERBEAN
by TOM BATIUK
Mom...
FLOWERS TOO?
YOU SHOULDN'T HAVE ...
WELL, SUMMER DOESN'T HAVE ANY MONEY, SO I FIGURED...
I ALSO PICKED THIS UP FOR YOU.
WHAT IS IT?
YOU'VE BEEN TALKING ABOUT TRYING TO GET IN TOUCH WITH THE SON YOU GAVE UP FOR ADOPTION WHEN YOU WERE IN HIGH SCHOOL...
THOSE ARE THE PAPERS YOU NEED SO YOU CAN FILE AN AFFIDAVIT ALLOWING THEM TO RELEASE YOUR IDENTITY.
HAPPY MOTHER'S DAY.
BATIUK

I TALKED WITH HOLLY AND SHE GAVE ME THE NAMES OF SOME OTHER ONCOLOGISTS TO CHECK OUT IN CASE YOU WANT TO SWITCH FROM DR. HALLETT.
I'VE THOUGHT ABOUT IT... AND THE MISTAKE WASN'T DR. HALLETT'S...
AND BESIDES, SHE'S GETTING ME INTO THAT CLINICAL TRIAL.
BATIUK
5-14
BUT THANKS FOR MAKING MY HORROR YOURS TOO.

IF I'M GOING TO BE STARTING AGAIN...
I GUESS I CAN SAY GOODBYE TO MY PEACH FUZZ.
BATIUK
WHO'D HAVE THOUGHT I'D MISS HAVING A BAD HAIR DAY?
5-15

Panel 1:
I'VE BEEN THINKING...

UH-OH... YOU HAVEN'T BEEN WATCHING THAT HOUSE MAKEOVER PORN ON TV AGAIN?

Panel 2:
NO... THIS IS ABOUT MORE IMMEDIATE CONCERNS.

5-16

Panel 3:
FOR STARTERS... I THINK IT'S TIME FOR ME TO TAKE A BREAK FROM MY LEGAL PRACTICE FOR AWHILE.

Panel 4:
IF I'M GOING TO BE STARTING CHEMO AGAIN...

I'LL FEEL LIKE CRUD, I'LL NEED MORE REST, AND THAT MEANS I'LL BE OUT OF THE OFFICE A LOT.

I JUST WON'T BE ABLE TO DO A GOOD JOB FOR MY CLIENTS.

I'LL MISS MY PRACTICE THOUGH.

COMPARED TO CHEMO...

BEING A LAWYER IS A WALK IN THE PARK.

5-17

159

WHAT'S THE OTHER THING YOU'VE BEEN THINKING ABOUT?
5-18
CONTACTING THE SON I GAVE UP FOR ADOPTION...
SO HE CAN HAVE ACCESS TO MY MEDICAL HISTORY.
I JUST DON'T WANT A GENETIC DISPOSITION FOR CANCER TO BE THE ONLY THING I EVER GAVE HIM.
BATIUK

SIGH
5-19
WELL, I GUESS I'D BETTER GET STARTED WITH MY 'RETIREMENT'!
BATIUK

FUNKY WINKERBEAN by TOM BATIUK

HOW'S THE 'RETIREMENT' COMING?

I'VE MOVED ALL MY CLIENTS OVER TO OTHER ATTORNEYS ... AND I'M ALMOST READY TO CLOSE UP SHOP.

I JUST HAVE A COUPLE OF LAWYER THINGS TO TAKE CARE OF.

I NEED TO MAKE OUT A DURABLE POWER OF ATTORNEY FOR LES ... AND PREPARE A LIVING WILL.

YOU KNOW, AS A LAWYER, I'VE WRITTEN LOTS OF LIVING WILLS FOR PEOPLE...

I JUST NEVER THOUGHT I'D BE WRITING MY OWN SO SOON.

JESS.
HEY, PETE! HOW ARE YA?
ME? WHO CARES HOW I AM!?
BMUK
I'M REALLY WORRIED ABOUT DARIN!
5-21

DO YOU KNOW HOW OBSESSED DARIN'S BECOME WITH THE SEARCH FOR HIS BIRTH PARENTS?
5-22
HE'S CHECKING THAT P.O. BOX ALL THE TIME!
OH, IT'S NOT THAT BAD...
JESS... HE'S EVEN GOING ON SUNDAYS!

OKAY, OKAY... I'LL TALK TO DARIN.
'IT'S IMPORTANT FOR HIM TO UNDERSTAND...'
'THAT THESE THINGS TAKE TIME.'
5-23

DARIN.
BLUE NILE
COFFEE HOUSE
DARIN, WHAT'S WRONG?
THIS IS WHAT'S WRONG!
OHIO Department of Health
5-24

LOOK AT THIS! I GOT MY BIRTH RECORDS...
BUT ALMOST EVERYTHING'S **BLACKED OUT!**
5-25
APPARENTLY, I DON'T HAVE THE **RIGHT** TO KNOW WHO MY BIRTH PARENTS ARE!
BATIUK

IT'S UP TO MY BIRTH MOTHER TO AUTHORIZE THE RELEASE OF HER PERSONAL INFO.
THAT MEANS I MIGHT NOT FIND OUT WHO SHE IS FOR MONTHS...
BATIUK
5-26
IF AT ALL...

Funky Winkerbean
by Tom Batiuk

Dear friends...

It appears that my last e-mail about my cancer being in remission was a bit premature.

It seems the lab got my scans mixed up with someone else's (hospitals, gotta love 'em).

Although I'm back on chemo, don't be a stranger. If it's not a good time, I'll simply say so, but we do like hearing from you.

Please keep me, Les and Summer in your prayers...

All religious denominations welcome.

5-27

ARE YOU SURE YOU WANT ME TO GO PLAY TENNIS WITH BULL?
GO... PLAY!
YOU NEED A BREAK.
MY MOM IS HERE AND I'LL BE FINE.
OH, ON YOUR WAY..
WOULD YOU DROP THIS OFF AT THE POST OFFICE FOR ME?
IT'S THE BIRTH MOTHER CONSENT FORM.
I'VE DECIDED TO TRY TO CONTACT MY SON.
6-18

HEY, MISTER MOORE!
DARIN...
HAVE YOU HEARD FROM ANY COLLEGES YET?
NADA SO FAR.
6-19
WELL, I'M SURE THAT YOU'LL BE HEARING FROM SOMEONE BEFORE TOO LONG.
POST OFFICE

NICE GAME, YOU CRUMB BUM.

6-20

I WAS DOING GREAT UNTIL YOU POINTED OUT THAT I COULD SEE IF MY SWING WAS CORRECT BY WATCHING MY SHADOW.

IT'S PROBABLY GOING TO TAKE ME THE REST OF THE SUMMER TO GET MY GAME BACK.

I'M COUNTING ON IT.

HOW'S YOUR ADOPTION COMING?

WELL, WE'VE FINALLY FINISHED JUMPING THROUGH ALL OF THE HOOPLAS...

NOW IT'S JUST A MATTER OF WAITING.

YOU OKAY?

HUH? YEAH...

6-21

HOW'S LISA DOING?
OKAY...
THE CLINICAL TRIAL SHE WAS HOPING TO GET INTO DIDN'T PAN OUT... SO THEY'RE GOING TO TRY SOME RADIATION ALONG WITH HER CHEMO.
6-22
I NEVER KNOW WHAT TO SAY AT TIMES LIKE THESE.
SOMETIMES I THINK I BELONG IN A WITLESS PROTECTION PROGRAM.
HEY, IF YOU CAN MAKE **ME** SMILE... YOU'RE DOING PRETTY GOOD.
BATIUK

I'M GONNA CLEAN YOUR CLOCK!
ARE YOU TRYING TO TICK ME OFF?
6-23
IF YOU GUYS NEED ANYTHING AND I FIND OUT YOU DIDN'T CALL ME...
I'LL BREAK YOUR ARM!
BATIUK

STILL NO WORD FROM YOUR BIRTH MOTHER, DARIN?
NADA...
ACTUALLY, I KIND OF KNOW WHAT IT'S LIKE TO BE ADOPTED...
BATIUK
6-25
WHEN I WAS LITTLE, MY SISTER ALLY TOLD ME THAT THE MAILMAN DROPPED ME OFF.

THIS IS MY STOP...
6-26
I'M DOING YARD WORK FOR THE MOORES THIS SUMMER.
SO YOU'VE GONE FROM CUTTING CLASS TO CUTTING GRASS.
CUTE.
BATIUK

I REALLY APPRECIATE YOUR HELPING WITH THE YARD, DARIN.

WHEN LISA GOT SICK, I STARTED TAKING OVER MORE AND MORE OF THE CHORES...

6-27

BUT LATELY THE CHORES HAVE STARTED TAKING OVER ME.

THERE'S LEMONADE IN THE FRIDGE IF YOU'RE THIRSTY.

I... I DON'T... WHAT AM I SUPPOSED TO SAY?

NO, PLEASE... DON'T DO ME ANY FAVORS.

YOU DO WHAT YOU HAVE TO DO... JUST PACK UP YOUR STUFF AND MAKE SURE YOU'RE GONE BY THE TIME I GET BACK...

6-28

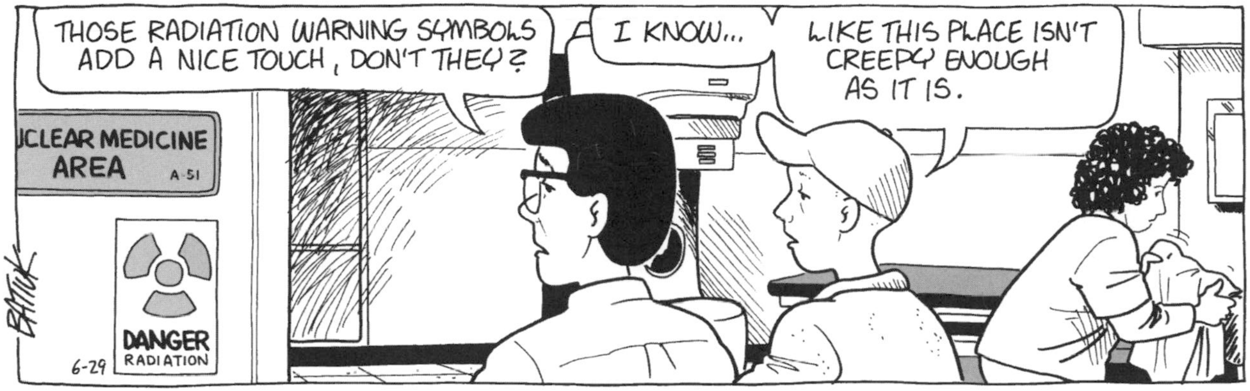
THOSE RADIATION WARNING SYMBOLS ADD A NICE TOUCH, DON'T THEY?
I KNOW...
LIKE THIS PLACE ISN'T CREEPY ENOUGH AS IT IS.
UCLEAR MEDICINE AREA A-51
DANGER RADIATION
BATIUK
6-29

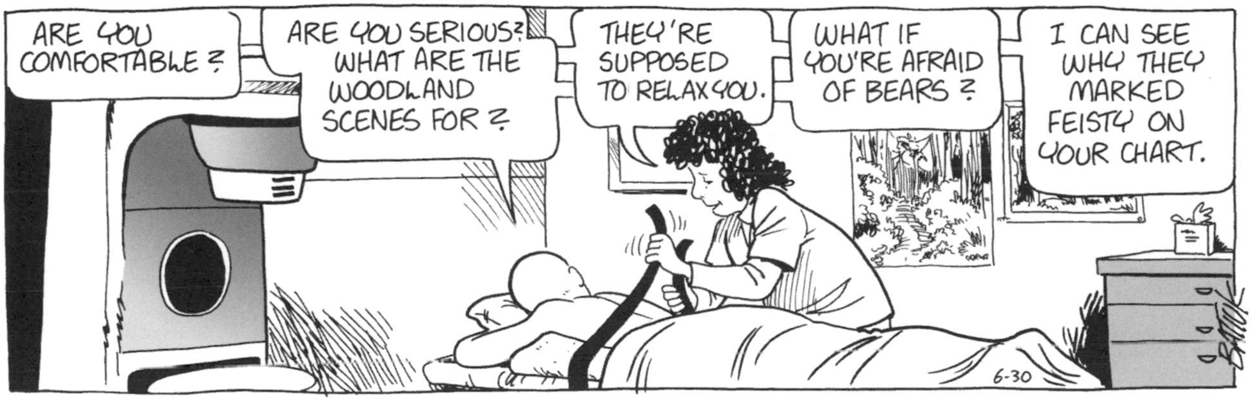
ARE YOU COMFORTABLE?
ARE YOU SERIOUS? WHAT ARE THE WOODLAND SCENES FOR?
THEY'RE SUPPOSED TO RELAX YOU.
WHAT IF YOU'RE AFRAID OF BEARS?
I CAN SEE WHY THEY MARKED FEISTY ON YOUR CHART.
6-30
BATIUK

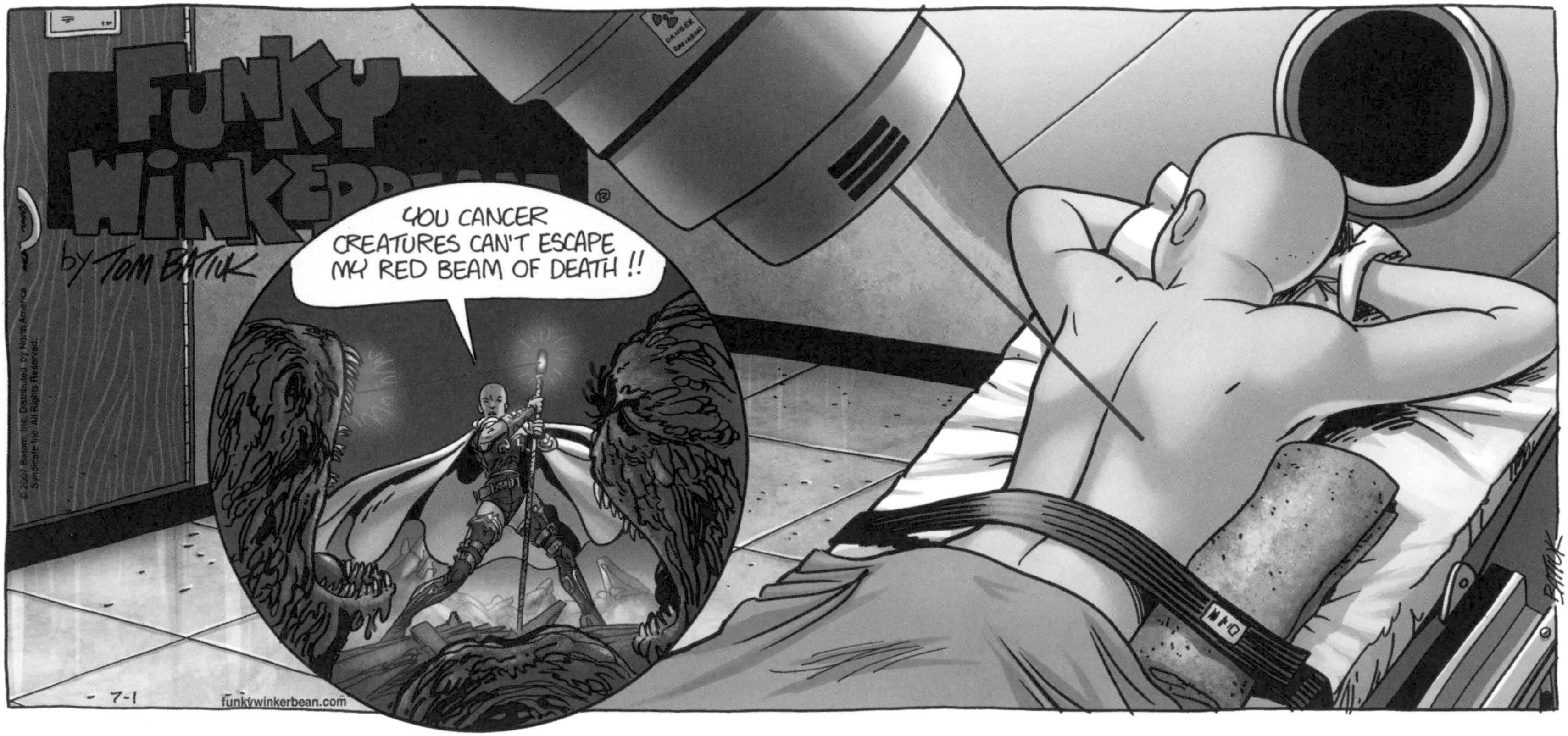
FUNKY WINKERBEAN
by TOM BATIUK
YOU CANCER CREATURES CAN'T ESCAPE MY RED BEAM OF DEATH !!
© 2007 Batom, Inc. Distributed by North America Syndicate Inc. All Rights Reserved.
7-1
funkywinkerbean.com
BATIUK

I'M AFRAID THE CANCER HAS CONTINUED TO PROGRESS AND IS IN AREAS WHERE SURGERY WON'T HELP.
WHAT ABOUT THE RADIATION?
THE RADIATION IS PRIMARILY INTENDED TO HELP RELIEVE PAIN...
NOT CURE...
7-2

SO WHAT ARE WE TALKING HERE?
DAYS?
NO...
YEARS?
NO...
MONTHS...
BUT DON'T ASK ME HOW MANY.
7-3

I'VE OFTEN WONDERED WHEN LIFE'S SENSE OF POSSIBILITIES WOULD END.
I NEVER REALIZED I'D BE ABLE TO CIRCLE THE DATE ON MY CALENDAR.

I'VE BEEN THINKING ABOUT THIS FOR AWHILE NOW... AND I'VE COME UP WITH A PLAN.
I'M GOING TO QUIT CHEMOTHERAPY.
WHAT DO YOU THINK?
I THINK YOU NEED A BETTER PLAN.

MAYBE THERE'S ANOTHER DRUG WE COULD TRY...
NO... I'M TIRED OF PUKING MY BRAINS OUT.
MY BODY JUST CAN'T TAKE THE ABUSE ANYMORE.
BUT YOU'VE ALWAYS BEEN A FIGHTER...
THIS IS A NEW FIGHT...
I WANT TO LIVE THE TIME I HAVE LEFT...
NOT JUST BE ALIVE.
7-6

STOPPING CHEMO...
I DON'T KNOW...
7-7
ARE YOU SURE YOU KNOW WHAT YOU WANT?
YES... I KNOW EXACTLY WHAT I WANT.
I WANT TO SEE THE LEAVES TURN ONE MORE TIME.

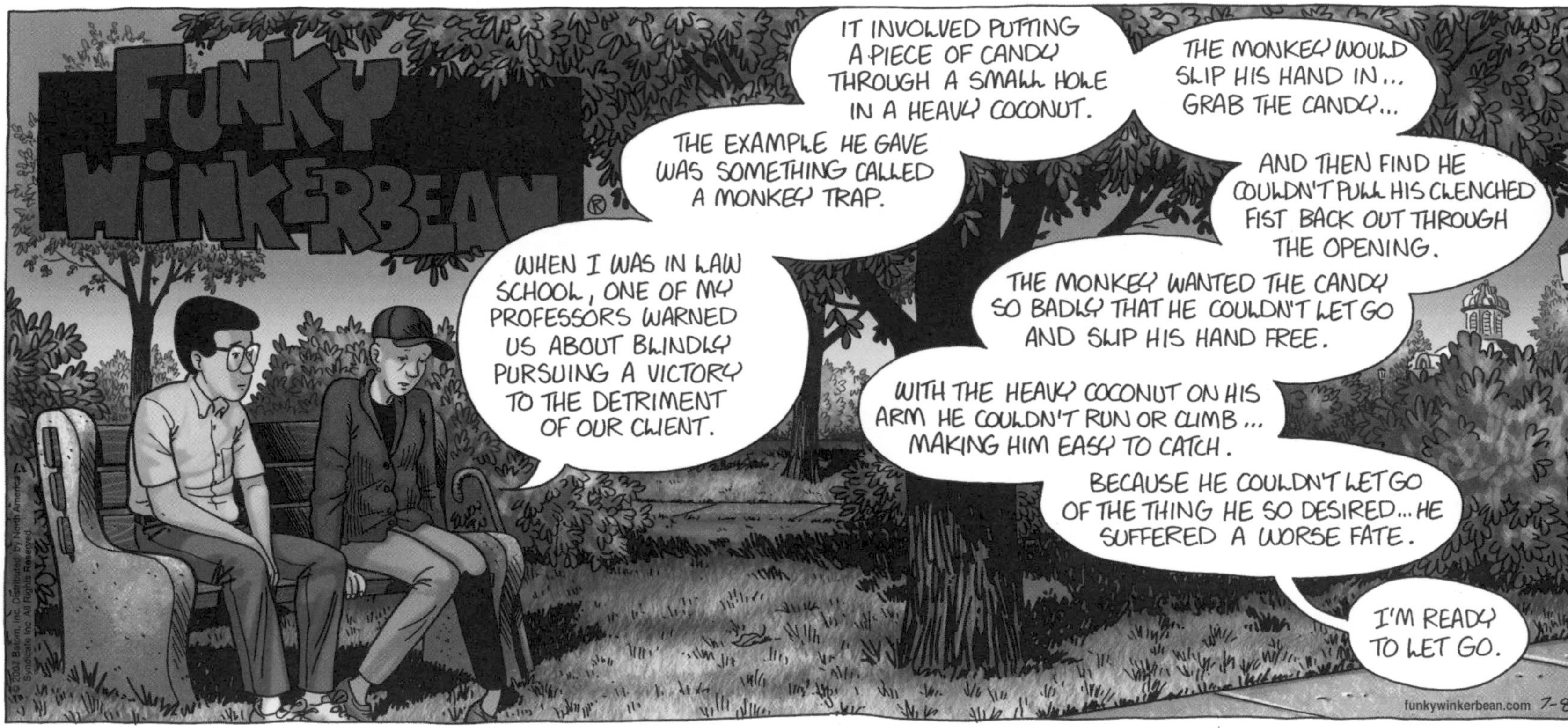
FUNKY WINKERBEAN
WHEN I WAS IN LAW SCHOOL, ONE OF MY PROFESSORS WARNED US ABOUT BLINDLY PURSUING A VICTORY TO THE DETRIMENT OF OUR CLIENT.
THE EXAMPLE HE GAVE WAS SOMETHING CALLED A MONKEY TRAP.
IT INVOLVED PUTTING A PIECE OF CANDY THROUGH A SMALL HOLE IN A HEAVY COCONUT.
THE MONKEY WOULD SLIP HIS HAND IN... GRAB THE CANDY...
AND THEN FIND HE COULDN'T PULL HIS CLENCHED FIST BACK OUT THROUGH THE OPENING.
THE MONKEY WANTED THE CANDY SO BADLY THAT HE COULDN'T LET GO AND SLIP HIS HAND FREE.
WITH THE HEAVY COCONUT ON HIS ARM HE COULDN'T RUN OR CLIMB... MAKING HIM EASY TO CATCH.
BECAUSE HE COULDN'T LET GO OF THE THING HE SO DESIRED... HE SUFFERED A WORSE FATE.
I'M READY TO LET GO.
funkywinkerbean.com 7-8

SO YOUR SCANS...?
WEREN'T SO HOT.
ONE OF THE TUMORS HAS GROWN FROM THE SIZE OF A PEA TO THE SIZE OF A PLUM.
MY DIAGNOSIS HAS GONE FROM SMALL VEGETABLES TO FRUIT.

ARE YOU REALLY SURE ABOUT GOING OFF CHEMO, LISA?
YES... WHY DOES EVERYONE KEEP ASKING ME THAT?
I WANT TO PLAY WITH SUMMER AND GO FOR WALKS WITH LES...
I DON'T WANT TO SPEND THE TIME I HAVE LEFT, ON MY KNEES BARFING UP THE BEST MODERN MEDICINE HAS TO OFFER.

LOOK, MY DOCTOR SAID THAT I COULD PICK UP THE CHEMO AGAIN AT ANY POINT...

BUT FOR NOW... IT'S GOING TO BE ABOUT THE LIFE I'M LIVING...

NOT THE LIFE I HAVE LEFT.

I'M FOR WHAT YOU WANT, AS LONG AS YOU'RE SURE...

I'M SURE... OKAY?

I'VE SAID THE WORD 'DIE'...

IT'S DONE...

IT'S OUT THERE!

I'D LIKE TO GET ON WITH LIVING NOW, THANK YOU VERY MUCH.

I DON'T KNOW WHERE SHE GETS HER STRENGTH, HOLLY.
IF IT WERE ME, I THINK I'D RATHER NOT SEE IT COMING.
7-13
LISA SEEMS TO HAVE ACCEPTED WHAT'S COMING.

I JUST WANT YOU TO KNOW THAT WE'LL BE HERE FOR YOU EVERY STEP OF THE WAY.
SNIFF
7-14
DAMN YOU... I WAS DOING FINE 'TIL YOU PULLED THAT.

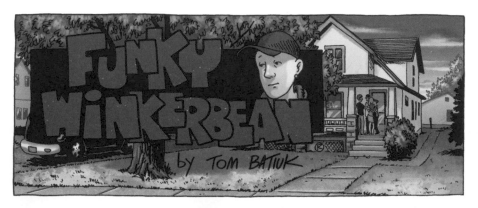

FUNKY WINKERBEAN

by TOM BATIUK

THANKS, YOU TWO...

WE'VE GOT THE BEST FRIENDS IN THE WORLD.

AND REALLY, I HAVE NO REGRETS...

EXCEPT FOR SMALL THINGS...

LIKE NEVER BEING ABLE TO SIT WITH LES AND WATCH THE BROWNS WIN A SUPER BOWL.

WELL, NONE OF US MAY EVER SEE THAT...

THIS HAS GONE ON TOO LONG, DARIN.

HAVE YOU **LOOKED** AT YOURSELF? YOU LOOK LIKE A **CORPSE!**

YOU **HAVE** TO STOP CHECKING THIS P.O. BOX!

IT'S TIME TO ACCEPT THE FACT THAT YOUR BIRTH MOTHER DOESN'T WANT TO CONTACT YOU.
I'M SO SORRY... IT'S MY FAULT.
I'M THE ONE WHO TALKED YOU INTO...
7-18
NO.
DON'T BE SORRY.

7-19
REALLY?
YEAH.

'NIGHT.
'NIGHT.
SLEEP TIGHT.
YOU TOO...
DON'T LET THE...
GET!
7-20

SEE YA, POST OFFICE.
POST OFFICE
7-21

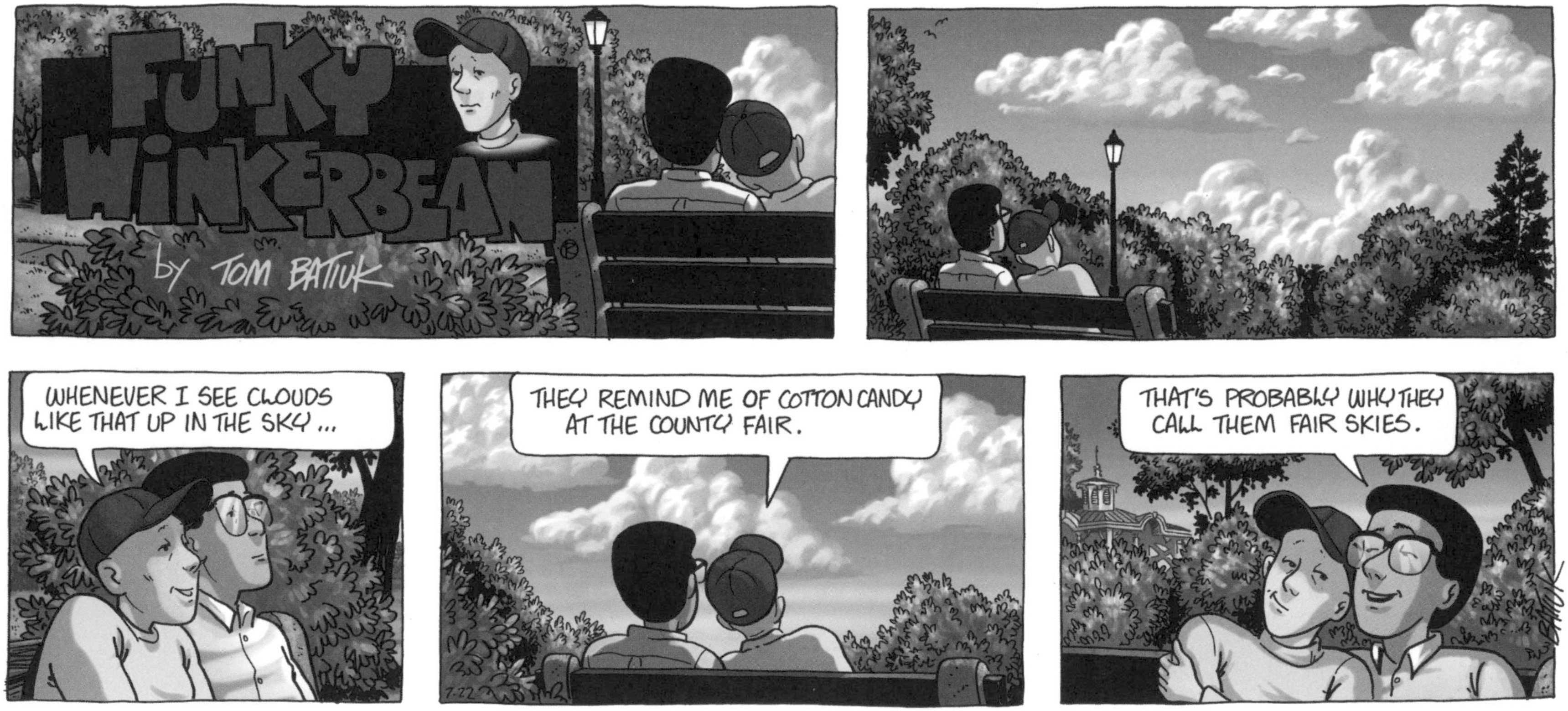
FUNKY WINKERBEAN
by TOM BATIUK
WHENEVER I SEE CLOUDS LIKE THAT UP IN THE SKY ...
THEY REMIND ME OF COTTON CANDY AT THE COUNTY FAIR.
7-22
THAT'S PROBABLY WHY THEY CALL THEM FAIR SKIES.

UH-HUH...
THANK YOU.

DARIN... I JUST GOT THE STRANGEST CALL.

YEAH? WHAT'S THAT?

7-23

DO YOU OWN A POST OFFICE BOX?

HERE YOU GO... PAID IN FULL, AND HERE'S THE KEY.

7-24

SEE YA.

HANG ON!

YOU FORGOT YOUR MAIL.

185

GEEZ... THAT'S A WHOLE LOTTA JUNK MAIL.
NNGH!
COME ON.
7-25

WHOA...
ODH
OHIO Department HEALTH
7-26

I'VE GOTTA...
BATIUK
OHIO Department of HEALTH
7-27

OHIO Department of HEALTH
Dear Darin:
I am very happy to inform you that your adoption search is now complete. Your birth mother has now filed an affidavit allowing me to release her identity, address and phone number to you. Your birth mother is
7-28
POS
OFFI
BATIUK

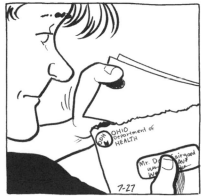

FUNKY WINKERBEAN
by TOM BATIUK
POST OFFI
ST OFFICE
AUTHORIZATION
FOR RELEASE - PARENT
OHIO DEPARTMENT of HEALTH
VITAL STATISTICS
ADOPTION
MOORE LISA
12 11 1988
Month Day Year
CRAWFORD LISA
AUTHORIZATION
FOR RELEASE - PARENT
OHIO DEPARTMENT of HEALTH
VITAL STATISTICS
ADOPTION
MOORE LISA
BATIUK
7-29

GET OUT!!
7-30
I'M NOT KIDDING, JESS...
MRS. MOORE IS MY MOM!

NOW THAT YOU KNOW WHO YOUR MOTHER IS, WHAT ARE YOU GOING TO DO?
7-31
I'LL TELL YOU WHAT I'M **NOT** GOING TO DO...
I'M NOT GOING OVER TO SEE HER...
BY MYSELF...

DARIN, WAIT...
ARE YOU SURE YOU WANT ME TO BE THERE WHEN YOU TELL MRS. MOORE YOU'RE HER SON?
BATIUK
8-1
I'VE NEVER BEEN MORE SURE OF ANYTHING IN MY LIFE.
OKAY, THEN.

8-2
BATIUK

THIS IS SO AMAZING!
I'VE ALWAYS WONDERED HOW MY SON WAS DOING...
AND NOW I FIND I'VE ALWAYS KNOWN!
I KNOW...
BATIUK
I'M SO GLAD YOU CAME WITH HIM, JESSICA...
JUST DON'T MAKE THE SAME MISTAKE THAT I DID...
BE SURE YOU'RE CAREFUL WHEN ... YOU KNOW...
WOW... SHE REALLY IS YOUR MOM.
8-3

WOW... I DIDN'T REALIZE HOW LATE IT WAS...
MY FOLKS WILL BE WONDERING WHERE I AM.
8-4
BEFORE I GO, IS THERE ANYTHING I CAN DO?
NO...
BATIUK
NOT UNLESS YOU'VE GOT A HEALTHY BODY STASHED AWAY SOMEWHERE.

FUNKY WINKERBEAN
by TOM BATIUK
AND AFTER INITIATING THE SEARCH...
I FOUND OUT LAST WEEK THAT MRS. MOORE IS MY BIOLOGICAL MOTHER.
I DIDN'T TELL YOU I WAS LOOKING FOR MY BIRTH MOTHER BECAUSE I DIDN'T WANT TO HURT YOU...
BUT I JUST WANT YOU TO KNOW...
MRS. MOORE MAY BE MY MOTHER...
BUT YOU'RE MY MOM.
8-5
BATIUK

WE'RE HERE BECAUSE I HAVE CANCER AND WE NEED TO TALK WITH OUR DAUGHTER, SUMMER, ABOUT...
Gathering place
A Caring Community for Those Touched by Cancer
8-6
AND WE DON'T KNOW HOW TO DO IT.
DON'T FEEL BAD...
MOST PEOPLE DON'T.
BATIUK

WHAT'S CANCER?
CANCER IS WHEN THE CELLS IN YOUR BODY GET SICK.
8-7
WHY DO THEY GET SICK?
WE'RE NOT SURE... BUT A LOT OF GOOD PEOPLE ARE TRYING TO FIND AN ANSWER.
BATIUK
I HOPE MY CELLS DON'T GET SICK.
ME TOO.

DOES CANCER HURT?
SOMETIMES IT DOES.
IS THAT WHY MOMMY CRIES?
YES... THAT'S PART OF IT.
8-8
WILL IT HURT IF I HUG YOU?
NO... THAT MAKES EVERYTHING FEEL BETTER.

ONE OF THE THINGS THAT BOTHERS ME MOST IS THAT I WON'T BE THERE FOR SUMMER AT THE BIG MOMENTS IN HER LIFE.
I WON'T BE ABLE TO TALK WITH HER WHEN SHE TURNS SIXTEEN...OR GOES TO HER FIRST PROM...
MAYBE YOU CAN...
8-9

WHEN I WAS A KID, I READ THE 'FOUNDATION' TRILOGY BY ISSAC ASIMOV.

IN IT, THIS PSYCHOHISTORIAN, HARI SELDON, MADE THESE HOLOGRAMS TO HELP GUIDE COMING GENERATIONS WHEN THEY WERE PLAYED FOR THEM IN THE FUTURE.

8-10

THERE'S NO REASON WHY YOU CAN'T DO THE SAME THING.

BEAM ME UP, SCOTTIE.

WAIT... THERE'S SOMETHING I HAVE TO DO BEFORE YOU START THE RECORDING.

SO SUMMER WON'T JUST REMEMBER ME SICK.

8-11

FUNKY WINKERBEAN
by TOM BATIUK ®
HAPPY SIXTEENTH BIRTHDAY, SUMMER.
I'M SURE THAT YOU'RE A BEAUTIFUL YOUNG WOMAN NOW.
REMEMBER THAT LIKE ALL WOMEN, YOU NEED TO TAKE CARE OF YOURSELF...
AND YOU SHOULD START GETTING REGULAR MEDICAL CHECK-UPS...
BECAUSE A CANCER CAUGHT EARLY CAN BE A CANCER CURED.
BATIUK
8-12
AND REMIND YOUR DAD THAT HE SHOULD BE CHECKING HIS PSA EVERY YEAR, TOO.

AND SO AS PART OF 'ONE VOICE AGAINST CANCER', I'LL BE GOING TO WASHINGTON...
TO TESTIFY BEFORE CONGRESS ABOUT THE CUTS THEY'VE MADE TO THE NATIONAL INSTITUTES OF HEALTH AND CANCER RESEARCH.
I'M SO GLAD YOU LET ME KNOW, HOLLY.
I KNEW YOU'D WANT TO HEAR ABOUT IT.
NO... I WANT TO GO WITH YOU.
8-13

TRAVEL TO WASHINGTON, DC?
I DON'T THINK YOU'RE REALLY UP TO THAT, LEESE.
PLEASE... LET **ME** DECIDE WHAT I CAN OR CAN'T DO.
8-14

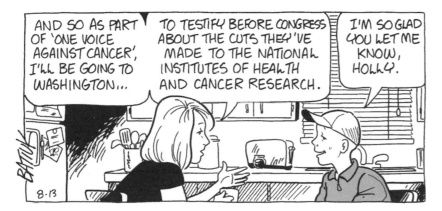

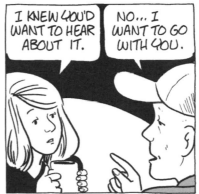

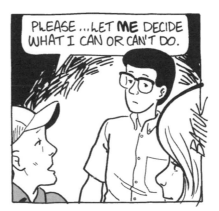

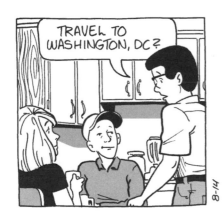

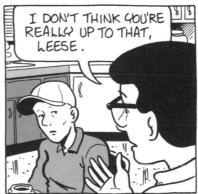

I'M NOT TRYING TO THINK FOR YOU, LEESE...
I JUST WORRY... THAT'S ALL.
I'VE JUST DECIDED THAT I'M NOT GOING TO ARRANGE MY LIFE FOR THE CANCER...
BATIUK
IT'S GOING TO HAVE TO ARRANGE ITSELF FOR ME.
8-15

MOMMY'S HAIR!
DID YOU WANT TO TAKE THIS?
NO... I'M LEAVING IT HOME.
BATIUK
I WANT OUR REPRESENTATIVES TO SEE WHAT I'M TALKING ABOUT.
8-16

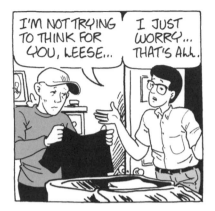

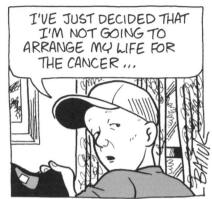

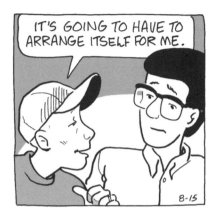

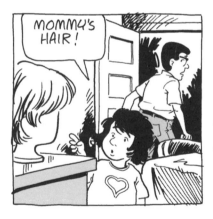

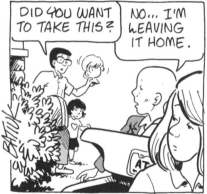

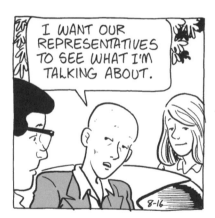

HERE'S WHERE WE'LL BE TESTIFYING.
THEY DON'T LOOK AS BIG AS THEY DO ON TV.
HEALTH AND HUMAN SERVICES SUB COMMITTEE
HEARING ROOM
BATIUK
THE HEARING ROOMS?
NO ... THE CONGRESSMEN.
8-17

MY NAME IS LISA MOORE.
I'M A WIFE, MOTHER AND, UNTIL A FEW WEEKS AGO AN ATTORNEY...
BATIUK
8-18
BUT I CAME HERE TO TALK TO YOU TODAY BECAUSE I HAVE CANCER.
MRS. MOORE

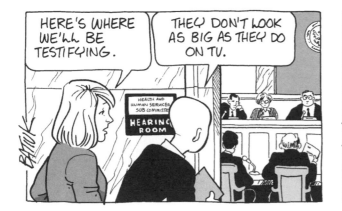

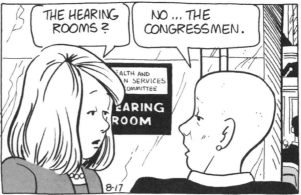

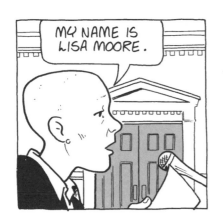

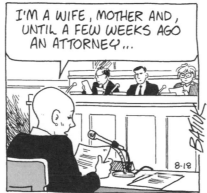

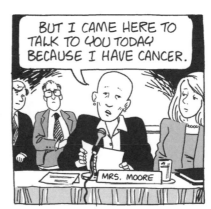

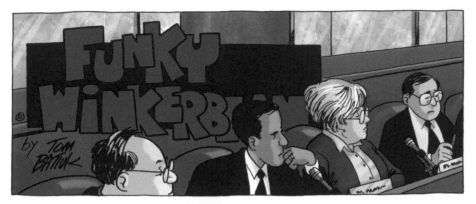

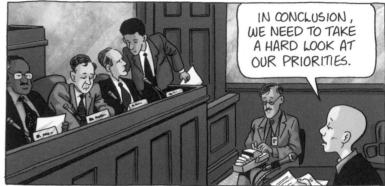

FUNKY WINKERBEAN
by TOM BATIUK
IN CONCLUSION, WE NEED TO TAKE A HARD LOOK AT OUR PRIORITIES.
AT A TIME WHEN WE'RE CLOSER THAN EVER TO BREAKTHROUGHS ON CANCER...
THE CONGRESS IS CUTTING BACK ON MONEY FOR RESEARCH.
8-19
BATIUK
WE CAN'T GIVE UP ON THE FIGHT NOW...
ESPECIALLY WHEN THIS IS A WAR WE CAN ACTUALLY WIN.

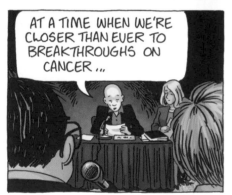

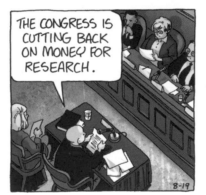

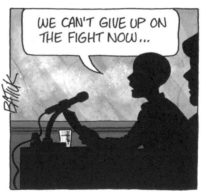

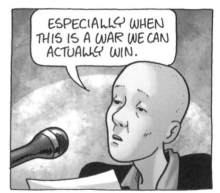

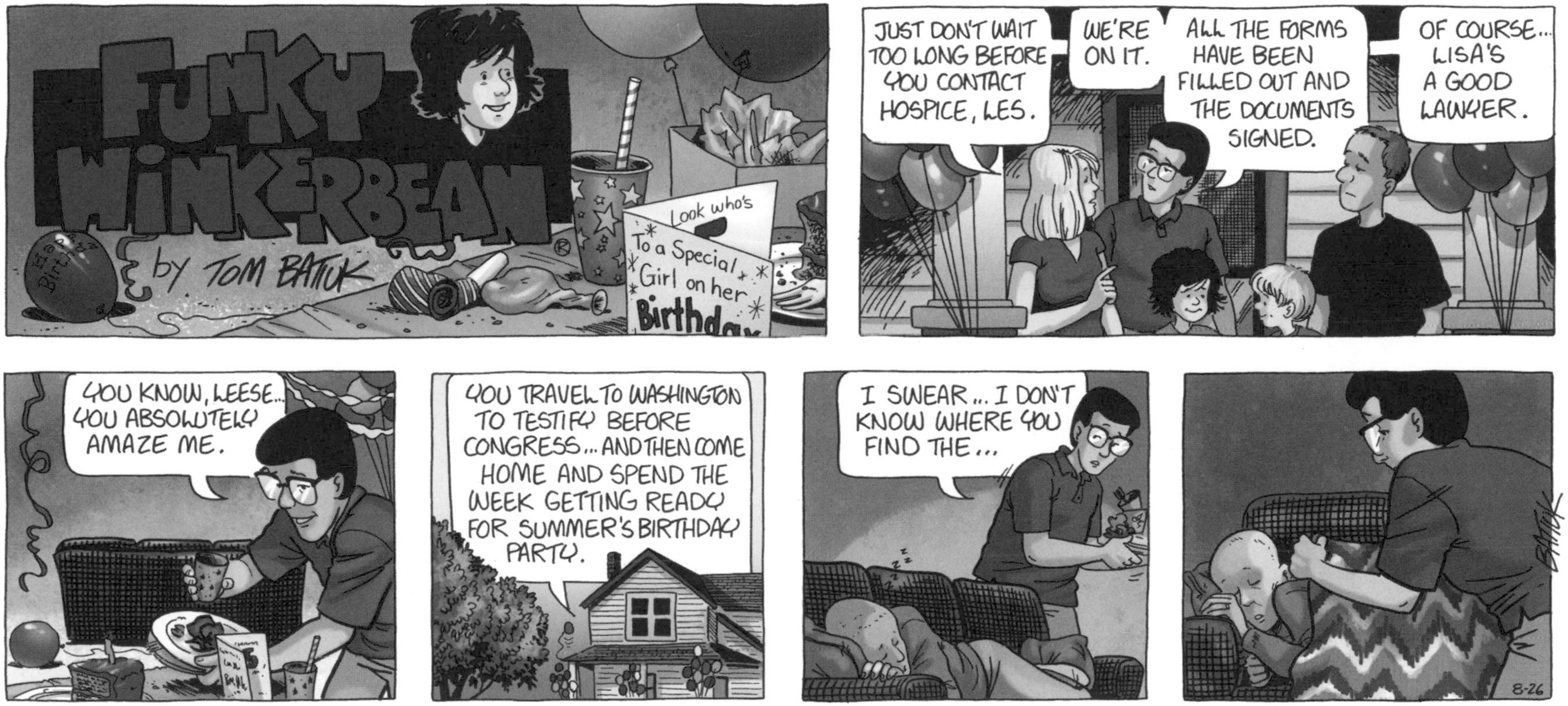
FUNKY WINKERBEAN
by TOM BATIUK
Look who's
To a Special Girl on her Birthday
JUST DON'T WAIT TOO LONG BEFORE YOU CONTACT HOSPICE, LES.
WE'RE ON IT.
ALL THE FORMS HAVE BEEN FILLED OUT AND THE DOCUMENTS SIGNED.
OF COURSE... LISA'S A GOOD LAWYER.
YOU KNOW, LEESE... YOU ABSOLUTELY AMAZE ME.
YOU TRAVEL TO WASHINGTON TO TESTIFY BEFORE CONGRESS... AND THEN COME HOME AND SPEND THE WEEK GETTING READY FOR SUMMER'S BIRTHDAY PARTY.
I SWEAR... I DON'T KNOW WHERE YOU FIND THE...
BATIUK
8-26

SEE? I TOLD YOU I'D WALK WITH YOU TO YOUR FIRST DAY OF SCHOOL.
SCHOOL
BE A BIG GIRL NOW... LOVE YOU.
8-27
I'LL WAIT HERE WHILE YOU GET THE CAR.
BATIUK

8-28
SO... SKIPPING RIGHT PAST THE HOT CHOCOLATE THESE DAYS?
BATIUK
NOTHING FOR LE CHAT BLEU?

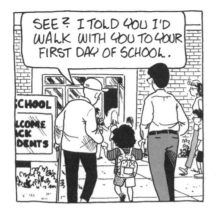

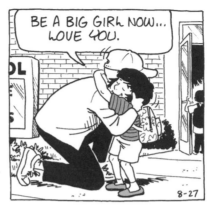

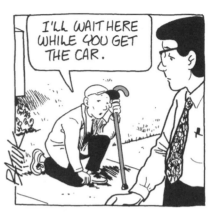

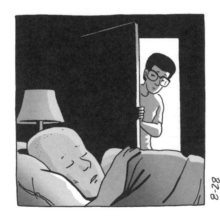

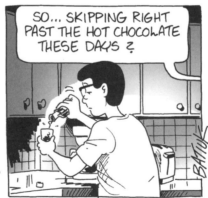

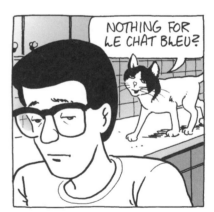

LE CHAT BLEU... JUST MY IMAGINATION'S WICKED WAY OF PERSONIFYING DEPRESSION.
WELL, I DON'T HAVE THE TIME FOR YOU RIGHT NOW.
THERE'S TOO MUCH THAT I HAVE TO TAKE CARE OF... TOO MUCH PRESSURE.
I DON'T HAVE TIME TO INDULGE YOUR PRESENCE.
NOT TO WORRY, CHER...
IT'S THE DECOMPRESSION THAT DOES YOU IN ANYWAY.
BATIUK
8-29

IN SICKNESS AND IN HEALTH ... 'TIL DEATH DO US FALL APART...
BATIUK
NO! IT'S NOT TIME FOR THAT YET!
FOR LISA?
8-30
OR FOR YOU?

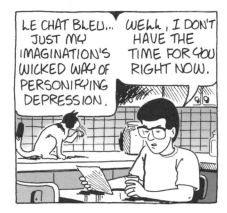

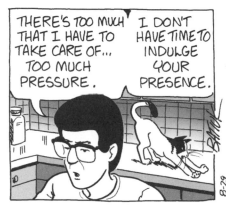

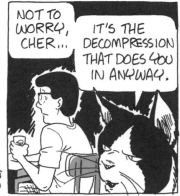

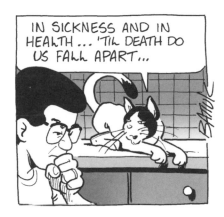

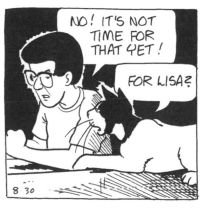

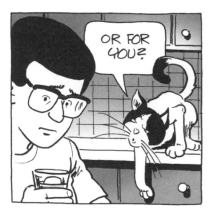

I JUST DON'T UNDERSTAND WHY LISA ISN'T FIGHTING THIS.
SHE'S ALWAYS BEEN SO STRONG.
SHE **IS** STRONG...
STRONG ENOUGH TO FACE THE TRUTH.
ARE YOU?
8-31

MMMM... CAN'T SLEEP?
I WAS JUST DOING SOME THINKING...
AND I JUST WANTED TO TELL YOU IT'S OKAY... OKAY FOR YOU TO GO.
9-1

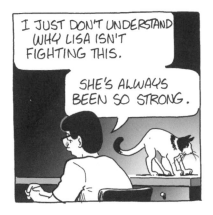

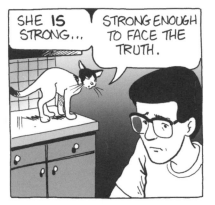

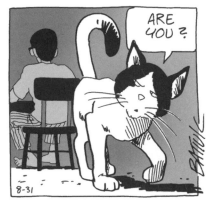

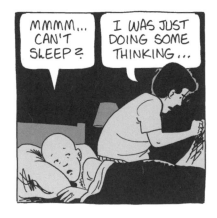

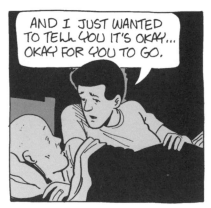

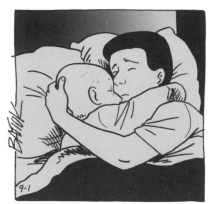

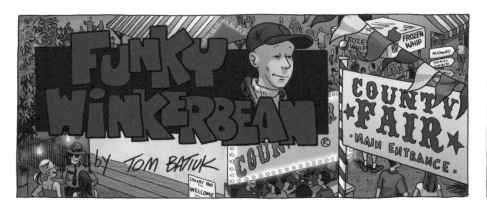

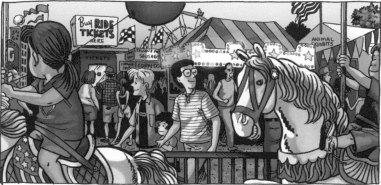

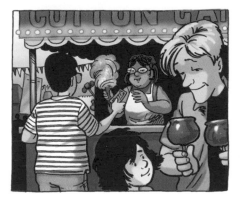

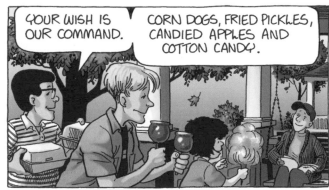

FUNKY WINKERBEAN
by TOM BATIUK
FROZEN WHIP
MIDWAY
COUNTY FAIR
•MAIN ENTRANCE•
COUNTY FAIR
WELCOME
Buy RIDE TICKETS HERE
TICKETS
SAUSAGE
ANIMAL EXHIBITS
YOUR WISH IS OUR COMMAND.
CORN DOGS, FRIED PICKLES, CANDIED APPLES AND COTTON CANDY.
ENOUGH SUGARS AND FATS TO SEND YOUR SPLITS OFF THE CHARTS.
HEY, IF I'M GONNA BE SENT OUT OF TOWN ANYWAY... I'M GONNA EAT WHAT I WANT.
9-2

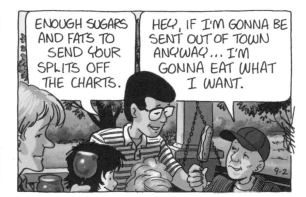

FUNKY WINKERBEAN
by TOM BATIUK
THANKS, DARIN... THE YARD LOOKS GREAT... HERE...
NO THANKS, MR. MOORE... I DON'T CHARGE FAMILY.
BEFORE I GO I HAVE SOMETHING FOR MRS... FOR MY MOTHER...
I THOUGHT YOU MIGHT WANT TO SEE THIS.
9-9
WHY DON'T WE WATCH IT TOGETHER?
BATIUK

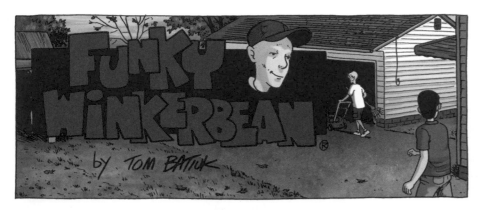

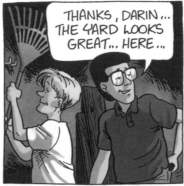

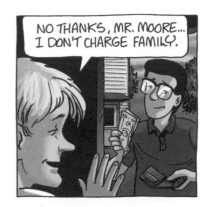

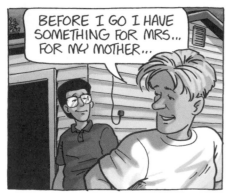

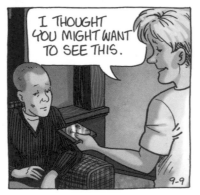

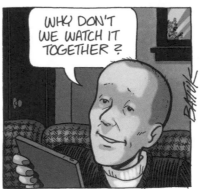

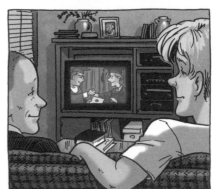

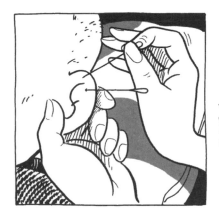

YOU ONLY NEED TO LEAVE THOSE NEEDLES IN YOUR EAR FOR ABOUT AN HOUR.

ATLAS OF ACUPUNCTURE POINTS

9-10

HEY, COOL WHERE DID YOU GET THOSE?

HOW DOES THAT FEEL?

BETTER...

9-11

BUT I'M NOT SO SURE I CAN MAKE IT UP THE STAIRS ANYMORE...

MAYBE IT'S TIME TO MAKE THE CALL.

207

THE BED WILL ALSO MAKE IT EASIER FOR HER TO BREATHE.
HOSPICE WILL HAVE A REGISTERED NURSE COME BY TOMORROW TO ADMINISTER A MORPHINE PATCH...
AND WILL THEN BEGIN FOLLOWING UP ON A REGULAR BASIS.
THANK YOU.
SO THIS IS THE NEW NORMAL.

ARE YOU SURE YOU WANT TO DO THIS, LEESE?
YES, I WANT TO GO TO THE PARK.
I WANT TO SEE IF ANY OF THE LEAVES HAVE STARTED TO TURN.

YOU KNOW, AFTER I'M GONE...

DON'T...

I'M JUST SAYING IT'S OKAY IF YOU FIND SOMEBODY ELSE...

AS LONG AS YOU GIVE IT AN ACCEPTABLE AMOUNT OF TIME...

9-14

SAY ABOUT TWENTY OR THIRTY YEARS.

I'D ALWAYS HOPED WE WOULD GET BACK TO NEW YORK SO YOU COULD TAKE ME ON THAT CARRIAGE RIDE IN CENTRAL PARK LIKE WE DID ON OUR HONEYMOON.

9-15

AFTER I'M CREMATED... I WANT YOU TO TAKE MY ASHES THERE AND SCATTER THEM IN THE PARK.

WHERE?

I DON'T KNOW... SURPRISE ME.

FUNKY WINKERBEAN
by TOM BATIUK
WHY IS MOMMY'S BED HERE?
BECAUSE MOMMY CAN'T GO UP AND DOWN THE STEPS ANYMORE.
MOMMY'S GOING TO SLEEP HERE ALL BY HERSELF?
YES, BUT WE'LL BE RIGHT UPSTAIRS.
BATIUK
9-16

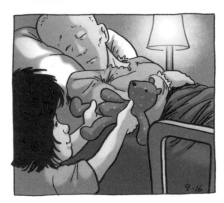

IS LISA UP FOR SOME VISITORS? SURE... SHE'D LOVE TO SEE YOU TWO.

9-17

MAKE THAT **THREE.**

WE'VE BEEN WORKING FOR A LONG TIME WITH AN ASIAN ADOPTION AGENCY... AND THE BIG DAY FINALLY ARRIVED.

SHE'S SO SWEET.

CONGRATS, YOU TWO.

9-18

THE PLANE WE FLEW IN ON WAS DELAYED FOR MECHANICAL REASONS... AND THEN OUR CAR BROKE DOWN ON THE WAY HOME...

SO WE'RE THINKING OF CALLING HER JINX.

BULL AND LINDA SEEM REALLY HAPPY.
YEAH... FROM WHAT BULL HAS SAID THEY MAKE A PRETTY GOOD TEAM.
9-19
THEY'RE IN A 5-2 DEFENSE AND THE LINE IS SLANTING RIGHT...
AND THE BACKERS ARE STUNTING...

LISA'S SYSTEMS ARE BEGINNING TO SLOWLY SHUT DOWN AS THE CANCER SPREADS THROUGH HER BODY.
OUR MAIN JOB NOW IS TO TRY TO KEEP HER PAIN FREE.
FROM YOUR EXPERIENCE, WHAT'S THE LAST THING TO GO?
9-20
LOVE.

HOUSE CLEANERS, CAREGIVERS, BABYSITTERS AND SHOPPING ASSISTANTS AT YOUR SERVICE.
BATIUK
9-21
THANK YOU.
DON'T THANK US YET... YOU HAVEN'T EATEN LINDA'S TACO LASAGNA.

THE HOSPICE NURSE GAVE ME A LIST OF THINGS THAT I NEED TO PICK UP.
COME WITH.
SHOPPING JUST HAPPENS TO BE MY AREA OF EXPERTISE.
9-22

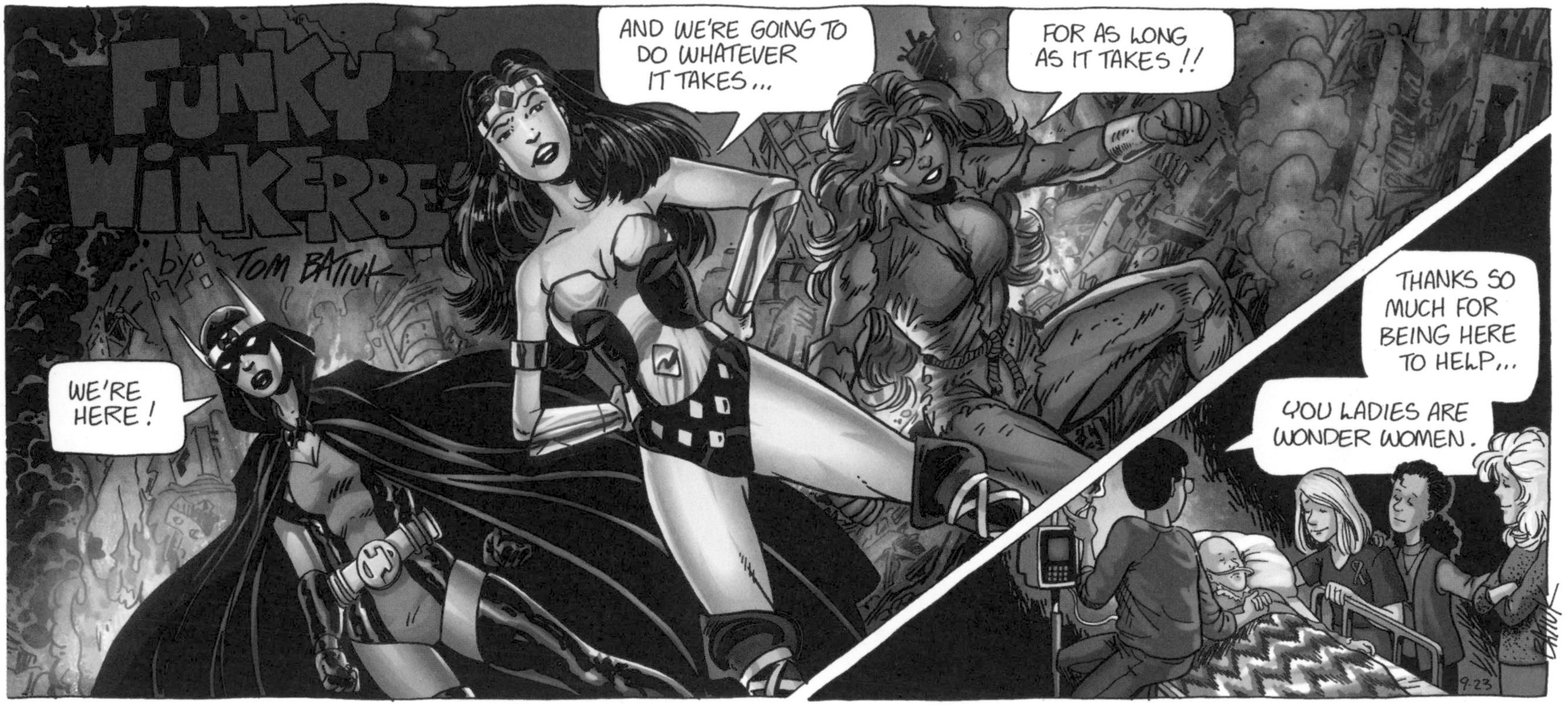
FUNKY WINKERBEAN
by TOM BATIUK
WE'RE HERE!
AND WE'RE GOING TO DO WHATEVER IT TAKES...
FOR AS LONG AS IT TAKES!!
THANKS SO MUCH FOR BEING HERE TO HELP...
YOU LADIES ARE WONDER WOMEN.
9-23

I THINK I WANT TO GET INTO BED.
OKAY... PUT YOUR ARMS AROUND MY NECK.
IT'S TIME FOR THE CAREGIVERS' MAMBO.
BATIUK
9-24

AHHH...
SORRY...
BATIUK
YOU ALWAYS WERE A LOUSY DANCER.
THAT'S BECAUSE YOU ALWAYS TRIED TO LEAD.
9-25

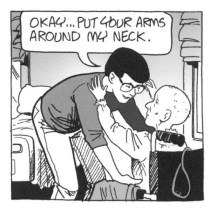

IS SHE...?
SHE'S JUST RESTING.
9-26
CAN SHE HEAR ME?
JUST TALK TO HER.

LISA... THERE'S SOMETHING I'VE WANTED TO TELL YOU...
BUT I COULD NEVER SEEM TO FIND THE RIGHT TIME...
9-27
I HOPE IT'S NOT TOO LATE.
WHAT IS IT, DAD?

I HAD SO MANY DREAMS FOR YOU WHEN YOU WERE A LITTLE GIRL... MY LITTLE GIRL...

I ALWAYS WANTED EVERYTHING TO BE PERFECT FOR YOU, YOU KNOW...? AND WHEN YOU BECAME PREGNANT IN HIGH SCHOOL... I LOST ALL OF THOSE DREAMS... AND I FELT I'D LOST YOU TOO...

AND THE ONLY WAY I COULD DEAL WITH THAT WAS TO SHUT IT OUT... SHUT YOU OUT...

9-28

I'M SO SORRY I SHUT YOU OUT... AND I'M SORRY FOR ALL THE TIMES I WAS SO ANGRY...

9-29

I'M SORRY FOR NOT BEING THERE WHEN YOU NEEDED ME...

PLEASE FORGIVE ME.

217

FUNKY WINKERBEAN®
by TOM BATIUK
MONTY
AAAACHOOOO
AND THEN MONTY SAYS...
YOU KNOW, LEESE... ONE OF THE THINGS I'VE ALWAYS LOVED WAS SITTING TOGETHER WITH YOU READING THE SUNDAY PAPER.
ESPECIALLY THE COMICS PAGES.
9-30
BECAUSE THEY ALWAYS MADE YOU LAUGH.
BATIUK
I GUESS THAT'S WHY THEY'RE CALLED THE FUNNIES.
WHS

WHERE ARE YOU!?
10-1
I'M RIGHT HERE...
BATIUK
I CAN'T SEE YOU!!

I CAN'T SEE THE LEAVES!
DID THEY TURN COLOR YET?
YES... THE MAPLE OUT FRONT IS A BLAZING YELLOW...
AND THEY'RE FORMING A GOLDEN CARPET ON THE LAWN...
AND TOMORROW WE'LL RAKE THEM INTO BIG PILES...
AND THEN WE'LL...
BATIUK
10-2
JUMP INTO THE PILES JUST THE WAY WE USED TO!

I DIDN'T MISS THE LEAVES...
NO.
10-3
OH...
IT'S TIME?

WAIT!
10-4
I LOVE YOU.
DID SHE SAY SOMETHING?
SHE'S GONE.

IMMEDIATELY AFTER LISA DIED... EVERYTHING WAS A BLUR OF PAPERWORK... THE FUNERAL HOME, HOSPICE, OBITUARIES, PLANNING A MEMORIAL SERVICE...

ALL OF WHICH I THREW MYSELF INTO NONSTOP... BECAUSE IF I STOPPED FOR EVEN A SECOND...

10-5

I'D START WONDERING IF I'D DONE EVERYTHING THAT I COULD HAVE DONE.

WE BURIED PART OF LISA'S ASHES AT THE FUNERAL SERVICE... AND I KEPT THE REST SO I COULD KEEP MY PROMISE TO HER...

'FOR AH MY HEART, HOW VERY SOON... THE GLITTERING DREAMS OF YOUTH ARE PAST...'

10-6

'AND LONG BEFORE IT REACHED ITS NOON, THE SUN OF LIFE IS OVERCAST.'

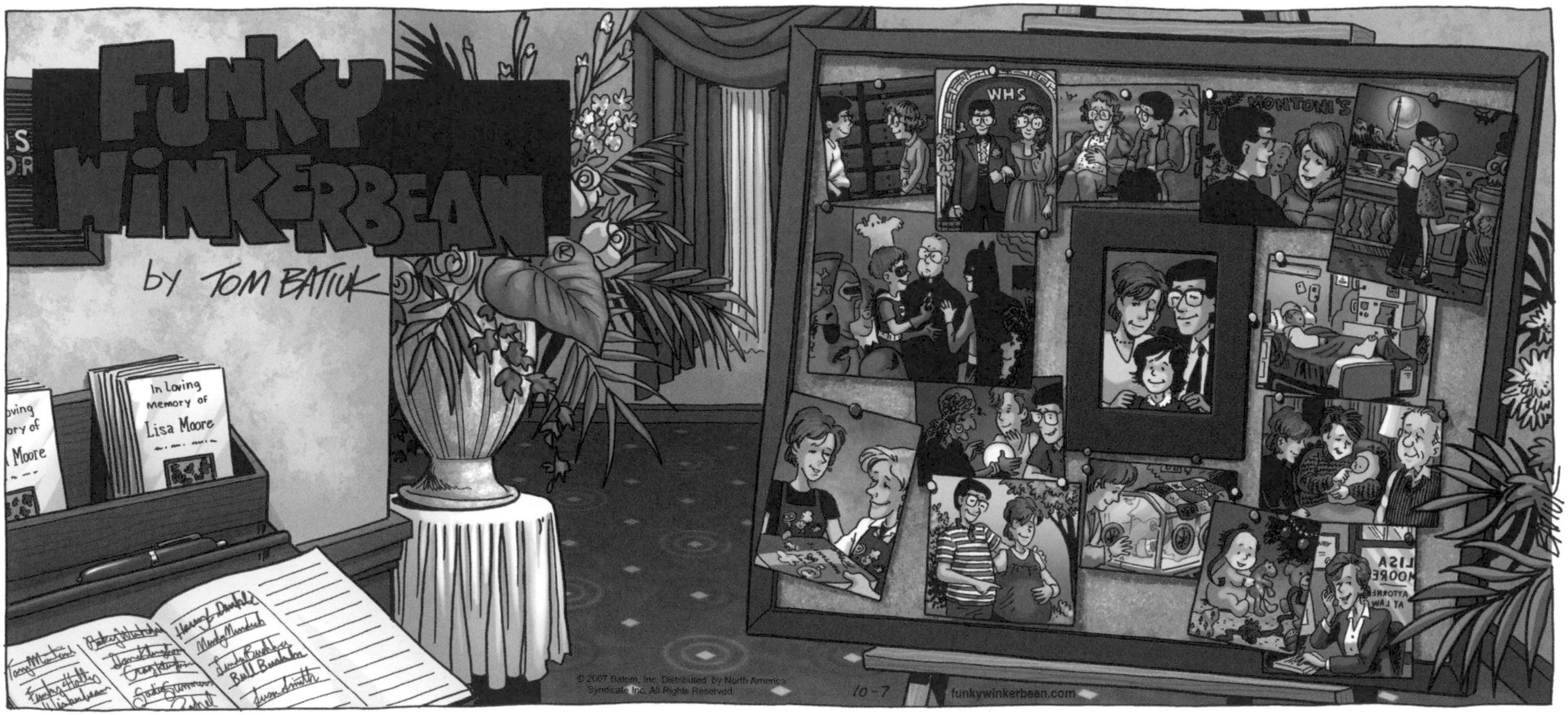
FUNKY WINKERBEAN
by TOM BATIUK
In Loving Memory of Lisa Moore
WHS
MONTONI'S
LISA MOORE ATTORNEY AT LAW
© 2007 Batom, Inc. Distributed by North America Syndicate Inc. All Rights Reserved
10-7
funkywinkerbean.com

IN MY GRIEF, MY ONLY CONCERN WAS KEEPING MY PROMISE TO LISA.
BATIUK
10-8

I WAS SO DISTRAUGHT OVER WHAT I'D LOST... THAT I ALMOST LOST EVERYTHING ELSE THAT MATTERED.
BATIUK
'THEY NEVER CHECKED THE CAMERA BAG WITH LISA'S URN AT THE AIRPORT.'
TO ALL GATES
10-9
1059
TAXI

MOORE
10-10
R RENT
721
SOLDIERS TAKEN HOSTAGE
10-11
WHOA... SORRY!
NEW & USED

SUMMER!
I TOLD HER I'D BE BACK TODAY! I'VE GOT TO GET...
Sunshine HOTEL
HOME...?
BATIUK
10-12

THIS IS OUR LUCKY CENTRAL PARK QUARTER...
IF WE EVER GET INTO A REAL JAM... IT'LL GET US OUT!
10-13
BATIUK

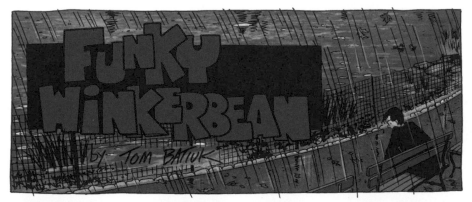

FUNKY WINKERBEAN by TOM BATIUK

HEY...

HEY,...

YOU REALIZE OF COURSE THAT AFTER THIS...

YOU HAVE TO GIVE ME A RIDE TO THE AIRPORT ANYTIME I WANT FOR THE REST OF MY LIFE.

IN THE END... SUMMER WAS THE LIFELINE THAT SLOWLY PULLED ME BACK INTO THE WORLD.

10-15

10-16

227

WHEN LISA WENT OUT... SHE WOULD ALWAYS LEAVE A NOTE FOR ME.
ONE TIME I CAME HOME AND SAW A PIECE OF PAPER SITTING ON THE TABLE IN THE KITCHEN...
AND FOR A MOMENT... I THOUGHT IT WAS A NOTE FROM LISA TELLING ME WHERE SHE'D GONE.

THERE WERE TV SHOWS THAT LISA WATCHED THAT I NEVER PAID THAT MUCH ATTENTION TO...
'BUT AFTER LISA DIED... I TOOK COMFORT FROM SITTING AND WATCHING HER FAVORITE SHOWS'.

10-19

WHEN'S MOMMY COMING HOME?
I CAN'T BRING HER HOME, SUMMER...
BUT I **CAN** TAKE YOU TO A PLACE THAT SHE LIKED TO GO.
10-20

FUNKY WINKERBEAN
by TOM BATIUK
AND SO THAT'S WHAT HAPPENS TO PEOPLE WHEN THEY DIE.
SO NOW DO YOU KNOW WHERE YOUR MOMMY IS?
10-21
YOU KNOW YOUR MOTHER WOULD REALLY BE PROUD...
OF THE YOUNG WOMAN YOU'VE BECOME.
BATIUK

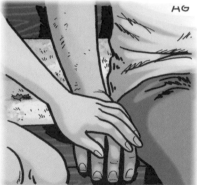

ACT III ~ Ten years later
SO THIS WAS WHERE YOU SCATTERED THE REST OF MOM'S ASHES?
MAKING STRIDES AGAINST CANCER
UH-HUH... THIS WAS ALWAYS HER FAVORITE PART OF CENTRAL PARK...
10-22
BATIUK
AND SHE WANTED TO BE IN A SPOT WHERE SHE COULD PEOPLE WATCH.

ACT III ~ Ten years later
SO YOU AND MOM CAME TO NEW YORK ON YOUR HONEYMOON?
10-23
YES... AND WE JUST KIND OF FELL IN LOVE WITH IT.
MAKING STRIDES AGAINST CANCER
BATIUK
LISA USED TO SAY THAT IF SHE SAT HERE AND CLOSED HER EYES... SHE COULD HEAR THE CITY BREATHE.

ACT III ~ Ten years later
WE'D BETTER SCOOT, KIDDO... THE 'MAKING STRIDES WALK' WILL BE FORMING UP IN A FEW MINUTES.
FOR LISA
10 24

ACT III ~ Ten years later
I'M GLAD WE CAME **HERE** THIS YEAR FOR THE 'MAKING STRIDES WALK', DAD.
WHICH REMINDS ME...
I'D BETTER GIVE BULL A CALL AND SEE HOW THINGS ARE GOING WITH OUR WALK BACK HOME.
MAKING STRIDES
NO WORRIES, LES... EVERYONE IS OFF AND WALKING, SAUNTERING, MOSEYING... YOU NAME IT.
MAKING STRIDES AGAINST CANCER
10-25

ACT III~Ten years later
IT'S JUST A BEAUTIFUL FALL DAY HERE, LES.
LISA WOULD'VE LOVED IT.
Lisa's Legacy
Making Strides Against Cancer Walk
MAKING STRIDES
MAKING STRIDES AGAINST CANCER
BATIUK
10-26

The beginning

Guide to Resource Materials

Breast Cancer Resources · Hospice and Palliative Care Resources ·
Resources for Health Care Professionals and Students

Breast Cancer Resources

Copyright 2007 by American Cancer Society. Reprinted by permission.

The American Cancer Society
1-800-ACS-2345
www.cancer.org
   Providing the public with accurate, up-to-date information on cancer is a priority for the American Cancer Society. The Society provides information on all aspects of cancer as well as the Society's programs and services through a toll-free information line, a Web site, and published materials.

National Breast Cancer Coalition
1101 17th St NW, Suite 1300
Washington DC 20036
Telephone: 800-622-2838
Fax: 202-265-6854
www.stopbreastcancer.org
   The National Breast Cancer Coalition is a grassroots membership organization whose mission is to eradicate breast cancer through action and advocacy.

National Cancer Institute
NCI Public Inquiries Office
6116 Executive Blvd
Room 3036A
Bethesda MD 20892-8322
Telephone: 800-4-CANCER (1-800-422-6237)
www.cancer.gov
   The National Cancer Institute, a component of the National Institutes of Health, supports and conducts groundbreaking research in cancer biology, causation, prevention, detection, treatment, and survivorship.

Susan G. Komen for the Cure
5005 LBJ Freeway, Suite 250
Dallas TX 75244
Helpline: 800-IM AWARE (1-800-462-9273)
Telephone: 972-855-1600
Fax: 972-855-1605
www.komen.org
   The Susan G. Komen Breast Cancer Foundation is an international nonprofit organization dedicated to eradicating breast

cancer as a life-threatening disease by advancing research, education, screening, and treatment.

Y-ME National Breast Cancer Organization
212 W Van Buren, Suite 1000
Chicago IL 60607-3903
Telephone: 312-986-8338
Fax: 312-294-8597
Hotline: 800-221-2141 (English, with interpreters for 150 languages); 800-986-9505 (Spanish)
www.y-me.org

Y-ME is a nonprofit organization serving men and women with breast cancer, as well as their families and friends. Its mission is to ensure, through information, empowerment, and peer support, that no one faces breast cancer alone.

Sharsheret
1086 Teaneck Rd, Suite 3A
Teaneck NJ 07666
Telephone: 866-474-2774
www.sharsheret.org

Sharsheret is a nonprofit organization of cancer survivors dedicated to addressing the challenges facing young Jewish women living with breast cancer.

American Breast Cancer Foundation
1220 B East Joppa Rd, Suite 332
Baltimore MD 21286
Telephone: 877-KEY-2-LIFE (877-539-2543)
Fax: 410-825-4395
www.abcf.org

The American Breast Cancer Foundation is a nonprofit organization dedicated to providing a fighting chance to every individual threatened by breast cancer, regardless of age, race, or financial challenge, through screening assistance programs, research, and support.

Mothers Supporting Daughters with Breast Cancer
25235 Fox Chase Dr
Chestertown MD 21620-3409
Telephone: 410-778-1982
www.mothersdaughters.org
MSDBC encourages those with Internet access to use the Web site rather than the phone number.

Mothers Supporting Daughters with Breast Cancer is a nonprofit Web-based organization providing support services specifically to help mothers with daughters battling breast cancer.

Men Against Breast Cancer
PO Box 150
Adamstown MD 21710-0150
Telephone: 866-547-6222 (Leave message for return call if answered by voice mail.)
Fax: 301-874-8657
www.menagainstbreastcancer.org

Men Against Breast Cancer is a nonprofit organization designed to educate and empower men to be effective caregivers when breast cancer strikes a loved one and to mobilize men in the fight to eradicate breast cancer.

Inflammatory Breast Cancer Research Foundation
321 High School Rd NE, Suite 149
Bainbridge Island WA 98110
Telephone: 877-786-7422
www.ibcresearch.org

The Inflammatory Breast Cancer Research Foundation is dedicated to the advancement of research in inflammatory breast cancer in order to find its causes and to improve treatment. The organization also seeks to increase awareness of symptoms of inflammatory breast cancer in the hope of leading to better clinical methods of detection and diagnosis.

Living Beyond Breast Cancer
10 East Athens Ave, Suite 204
Ardmore PA 19003
Telephone: 888-753-5222
www.lbbc.org

Living Beyond Breast Cancer is a national nonprofit education and support organization dedicated to empowering all women affected by breast cancer to live as long as possible with the best quality of life.

Inflammatory Breast Cancer Association
www.ibchelp.org

Inflammatory Breast Cancer Association is a Web-based organization that provides information specific to inflammatory breast cancer patients.

National Breast and Cervical Cancer Early Detection Program
Centers for Disease Control and Prevention
Division of Cancer Prevention and Control
4770 Buford Hwy NE, MS K-64
Atlanta GA 30341-3717
Telephone: 800-232-4636 (select Option 1, "General Health Information")
Fax: 770-488-4760
www.cdc.gov/cancer/nbccedp

The National Breast and Cervical Cancer Early Detection Program (NBCCEDP) provides screening services, including clinical breast examination, mammograms, pelvic examination, and Pap tests, to women underserved in the health care community. The NBCCEDP also funds postscreening diagnostic services, such as surgical consultation and biopsy, to ensure that all women with abnormal results receive timely and adequate referrals.

WomenStories
1807 Elmwood Ave
Buffalo NY 14207
Telephone: 716-873-3689; toll-free: 800-775-5790
Fax: 716-873-5361
www.womenstories.org

WomenStories, a nonprofit organization, benefits those who have been diagnosed with breast cancer and need the information and comfort that only other breast cancer survivors can provide. WomenStories is a series of videos in which breast cancer survivors offer emotional support.

Sisters Network™ Inc.
8787 Woodway Dr, Suite 4206
Houston TX 77063
Telephone: 713-781-0255; toll-free: 866-781-1808
Fax: 713-780-8998
www.sistersnetworkinc.org

Sisters Network™ Inc. is a national African American breast cancer survivorship organization. This nonprofit organization is committed to increasing local and national attention on the devastating impact that breast cancer has on the African American community.

Young Survival Coalition
61 Broadway, Suite 2235
New York NY 10006
Telephone: 646-257-3000; toll-free: 877-972-1011
Fax: 646-257-3030
www.youngsurvival.org

The Young Survival Coalition is dedicated to the concerns and issues that are unique to women aged 40 and younger with breast cancer.

SHARE: Self Help for Women with Breast or Ovarian Cancer
1501 Broadway, Suite 704A
New York NY 10036
Telephone: 212-719-0364
Toll-free breast cancer hotline and Spanish-speaking hotline: 866-891-2392
Fax: 212-869-3431
http://sharecancersupport.org

SHARE: Self Help for Women with Breast or Ovarian Cancer serves women, men, and children who have been affected by breast cancer or ovarian cancer. Services include hotlines, survivor support groups, public education, advocacy, and wellness programs.

FORCE: Facing Our Risk of Cancer Empowered
16057 Tampa Palms Blvd West, PMB 373
Tampa FL 33647
Telephone: 954-255-8732; toll-free: 866-824-7475
Fax: 954-827-2200
www.facingourrisk.org

Facing Our Risk of Cancer Empowered is a nonprofit organization for individuals and families affected by hereditary breast cancer and ovarian cancer due to the BRCA mutation or a family history of these cancers.

National Women's Health Information Center
8270 Willow Oaks Corporate Dr
Fairfax VA 22031
Telephone: 800-994-9662
www.womenshealth.gov

The National Women's Health Information Center (NWHIC) is a service of the Office on Women's Health in the Department of Health and Human Services. NWHIC provides a gateway to the vast array of federal and other women's health information resources.

National Asian Women's Health Organization
1 Embarcadero Center, Suite 500
San Francisco CA 94111
Telephone: 415-773-2838
Fax: 415-773-2872
www.nawho.org

National Asian Women's Health Organization is a national nonprofit health organization whose mission is to achieve health equity for Asian women and their families.

Patient Access Network Foundation
PO Box 221858
Charlotte NC 28222-1858
Telephone: 866-316-7263
www.patientaccessnetwork.org
Patient Access Network Foundation encourages those with Internet access to use the Web site rather than the toll-free number.

Patient Access Network Foundation is an independent, nonprofit organization dedicated to assisting underinsured patients who cannot afford the out-of-pocket medication costs associated with their treatment. Patients must be U.S. residents and meet certain financial, insurance, and medical criteria. In addition, the drugs must be covered by the patient's insurance.

Hospice and Palliative Care Resources

Prepared by the National Hospice and Palliative Care Organization (NHPCO), the largest nonprofit membership organization representing hospice and palliative care programs and professionals in the United States. Founded in 1978, NHPCO continues to break new ground in professional leadership, consumer and caregiver services, research, legislative advocacy, international development, and issues relating to quality care.

General Resources

Find information on advance care planning and living wills, pain control, financial issues, hospice and palliative care, and grief and loss.

Caring Connections
Helpline: 800-658-8898
www.caringinfo.org

Caring Connections is a program of the National Hospice and Palliative Care Organization (NHPCO), the largest nonprofit membership organization representing hospice and palliative care programs and professionals in the United States. The organization's mission is to lead and mobilize social change for improved care at the end of life. It is supported by a grant from The Robert Wood Johnson Foundation.

Caregiving and Home Care

Find information, support, tips, and medical assistance for taking care of loved ones at home.

American Association for Homecare
Telephone: 703-836-6263
www.aahomecare.org

Family Caregiver Alliance
Telephone: 800-445-8106
www.caregiver.org

National Family Caregivers Association
Telephone: 800-896-3650
www.nfcacares.org

Support Team Network
Telephone: 877-614-9129
www.supportteam.org

Visiting Nurses Association of America
Telephone: 888-866-8773 ext. 221
www.vnaa.org

Nursing Homes and Assisted Living

For help with finding a nursing home or assisted-living facility.

The American Health Care Association
Telephone: 202-842-4444
www.longtermcareliving.com

The Assisted Living Federation of America
Telephone: 703-849-1805
www.alfa.org

National Center for Assisted Living
Telephone: 202-842-4444
www.ncal.org

National Citizens Coalition for Nursing Home Reform
Telephone: 202-332-2276
www.nursinghomeaction.org

Pain Management, Chronic and Malignant

Find organizations that can help you learn about different types of pain and assist you in finding the pain treatment.

American Pain Society
Telephone: 847-375-4715
www.ampainsoc.org

Pain.com
www.pain.com

Cancer Pain
www.cancer-pain.org

American Pain Foundation
Telephone: 888-615-PAIN (888-615-7246)
www.painfoundation.org

The National Foundation for the Treatment of Pain
Telephone: 713-862-9332
www.paincare.org

Transportation

For patients who need to be treated at a facility a great distance from their homes.

Angel Flight
Telephone: 877-247-5433
www.angelflight.com

National Patient Travel Helpline
Telephone: 800-296-1217

MMA-Mercy Medical Airlift
Telephone: 888-675-1405
www.mercymedical.org

Organ Donation

Find information on how to become an organ donor, how the organ donation network works, and other national resources relating to organ donation.

United Network for Organ Sharing
Telephone: 888-894-6361
www.unos.org

Anatomy Gifts Registry
Anatomy Gifts Registry is a nonprofit corporation that provides an alternative to traditional funerals while supporting medical science and education.
Telephone: 800-300-5433

Hospice

Find a hospice or find information on patient advocacy, education, or technical assistance.

National Hospice and Palliative Care Organization
Telephone: 800-658-8898
www.nhpco.org

American Hospice Foundation
Telephone: 202-223-0204
www.americanhospice.org

Hospice Foundation of America
Telephone: 202-638-5419 or 202-638-5312
www.hospicefoundation.org

Children's Hospice International
Telephone: 800-24-CHILD (800-242-4453)
www.CHIonline.org

Partnership for Parents
www.partnershipforparents.org (English)
www.padrescompadres.org (Spanish)

Grief

Find support groups and information on the bereavement process.

National Hospice and Palliative Care Organization
Telephone: 1-800-658-8898
www.nhpco.org

The Dougy Center for Grieving Children and Families
www.dougy.org

The Compassionate Friends, Inc.
www.compasionatefriends.org

Journey of Hearts
www.journeyofhearts.org/

Resources for Health Care Professionals and Students

Prepared by John E. Selickman, medical student, Northeastern Ohio Universities College of Medicine, and Steven Radwany MD, Summa's Palliative Care and Hospice Services, Akron, Ohio.

Internet Resources

The amount of material on the World Wide Web related to end-of-life care is rapidly increasing. The references listed here, some of the largest Web sites dedicated to hospice and palliative care, were chosen because they met three simple criteria: are accredited organizations at the national level, act as gateways to many other related sites, and update their sites on a regular basis.

American Academy of Hospice and Palliative Medicine
www.aahpm.org
The AAHPM offers one of the best Internet resources available. Of particular interest are extensive listings and descriptions of educational materials (including books, articles, videos, and CDs); a "fast facts" section, with peer-reviewed one-page summaries on current topics in hospice and palliative medicine; and

a thorough listing of related sites. Also available are job listings in palliative and hospice care, a directory of all the palliative care fellowship programs in the country, and even a database to locate speakers for educational programs.

American Hospice Foundation
www.americanhospice.org

The American Hospice Foundation offers an extensive list of free informative articles on hospice-related issues as well as a directory of hospice programs in the United States, publications and brochures for sale, and a large section dedicated to managing grief. It also contains a unique section on end-of-life legal issues and a list of attorneys that specialize in them.

Center to Advance Palliative Care
www.capc.org

This site is dedicated to educating health care professionals on palliative care and to providing assistance to start and maintain palliative care programs across the country. It has helpful educational links for professionals as well as job openings, seminar listings, training opportunities, and an impressive collection of research and references on designing, maintaining, strengthening, and defending palliative care programs.

Growth House
www.growthhouse.org

Growth House contains one of the most comprehensive listings of Web sites dedicated to end-of-life care and terminal illnesses. In addition to its links, it also has a "bookstore" linked to amazon.com, which recommends and summarizes helpful reading material. Growth House Radio provides streaming music channels as well as educational programs.

Hospice Foundation of America
www.hospicefoundation.org

This organization's Web site has articles, reading lists, stories, and frequently asked questions on topics concerning hospice care. Also of interest are its monthly newsletter "Journeys" and a section that specifically addresses the concerns of familial care givers.

National Hospice and Palliative Care Organization
Helpline: 800-658-8898
www.nhpco.org

The NHPCO has put together a website unparalleled in its on-line resources for professionals and consumers. Its "Marketplace" section has one of the largest selections of hospice/palliative care books, videos, brochures, audio conferences on CD, and technical materials available for sale on the Internet. Marketplace Catalog 820540 has a variety of useful publications designed to assist professionals with end-of-life care issues. Available at www.nhpco.org/marketplace. The LIVE Campaign Resources for community outreach on end-of-life care issues are available at www.LIVEpartners.org.

Promoting Excellence in End-of-Life Care
www.promotingexcellence.org

This site provides resources for professional health care givers. Most of the resources are actually links to other Web sites, journal articles, books, and reports, although there has clearly been a good deal of effort finding and organizing them. This is most evident in the sections on "promoting excellence tools" and "key clinical assessment and research tools," each of which contains a large variety of forms, scales, and pamphlets.

Annotated Print Material

Textbooks

Ferrell, Betty R., and Nessa Coyle, eds. 2006. *Textbook of Palliative Nursing,* 2d ed. New York: Oxford University Press.

Aside from the target audience, this text is very similar to the *Oxford Textbook of Palliative Medicine* (below) in its scope, the amount of material covered, its research-based and experience-based grounding, and its arrangement. In particular, it tries to incorporate the humanity of palliative medicine: each chapter includes relevant case studies as well as an introductory quotation from a patient or family member dealing with the material covered.

Doyle, Derek, Geoffrey Hanks, and Nathan Cherny, eds. 2005. *Oxford Textbook of Palliative Medicine,* 3d ed. New York: Oxford University Press.

This textbook has become the definitive text on palliative medicine. Based on research and clinical experience, it is divided into broadly themed sections that include everything from symptom management to cultural and spiritual aspects of palliative medicine; each is divided into subsections written by contributing authors who represent expertise in their respective fields. The text is written to be universal, outlining basic principles as well as advanced techniques, and is geared specifically toward medical doctors.

Berger, Ann M., Russell K. Portenoy, and David E. Weissman, eds. 2002. *Principles and Practice of Palliative Care and Supportive Oncology,* 2d ed. Philadelphia: Lippincott, Williams, and Wilkins.

This text is similar to the two above; however, notable differences include the various perspectives brought by a list of almost entirely different contributing authors and information weighted more heavily toward palliative treatment for patients with malignant disease.

Pocket Guides and Handbooks

Watson, Max, Caroline Lucas, and Andrew Hoy. 2005. *The Oxford Handbook of Palliative Care.* New York: Oxford University Press.

Based on the third edition of the *Oxford Textbook of Palliative Medicine,* this handbook is intended for use by doctors, nurses, and allied health professionals. To facilitate quick reference, material is often repeated at multiple points (alongside relevant material). It includes nearly 200 blank pages for personal notes, further reading suggestions, and ribbon bookmarkers bound to the spine.

Storey, Porter. 2004. *Primer of Palliative Care.* Glenview, IL: American Academy of Hospice and Palliative Medicine.

Considerably more condensed than the *Oxford Handbook,* this text is also a fraction of the size and very conducive to quick use. Its target audiences are physicians in residency training, practicing physicians, and palliative care teams. Focusing primarily on pain and symptom management, it contains many tables that feature treatment and dosage suggestions.

Storey, Porter, Carol Knight, and Ronald Schonwetter. 2003. *Pocket Guide to Hospice and Palliative Medicine.* Glenview, IL: American Academy of Hospice and Palliative Medicine.

Case Studies

Macdonald, Neil, Doreen Oneschuk, and Neil Hagen, eds. 2005. *Palliative Medicine: A Case-based Manual,* 2d ed. New York: Oxford University Press.

This up-to-date second edition features multifaceted case studies on both malignant and chronic nonmalignant illnesses. It is an excellent resource for medical students, outlining at the opening of each chapter the attitudes, skills, and knowledge that the author intends to impart. Each case features multiple open-ended questions (in some cases more than 10) that are discussed in full by the contributing author. Most chapters also end with a small section discussing relevant future research.

Regnard, Claud, ed. 2004. *Helping the Patient with Advanced Disease.* Abingdon, UK: Radcliffe Medical Press Ltd.

This workbook contains more than 60 worksheets dealing with such topics as symptom and pain management, communication, and bereavement, among many others. Created with the idea of a "coffee update" in mind, worksheets take about 15 minutes to complete and involve a case study and information sheet, both multiple-choice and open-ended questions, and further reading suggestions. The difficulty of these worksheets ranges from introductory to advanced, and they are intended for use by health care professionals.

Storey, Porter, and Carold F. Knight. 2003. *American Academy of Hospice and Palliative Medicine Hospice/Palliative Care Training for Physicians: A Self-Study Program.* New Rochelle, NY: Mary Ann Liebert, Inc.

Eight booklets (ca. 100 pages each) comprise this series, which is meant to serve as an introductory text for physicians training in palliative care. Each booklet covers specific issues in depth (e.g., ethical and legal decision making, alleviating psychological and spiritual pain, etc.), contains a pre-test and post-test, and features clinical situations and references. The series serves as an excellent preparatory tool for the American Board of Hospice and Palliative Medicine's written examination for certification.

Enck, Robert E. 2002. *The Medical Care of Terminally Ill Patients,* 2d ed. Baltimore: Johns Hopkins University Press.

This book provides information on pain and symptom management by reviewing clinical studies related to end-of-life care at the time of its publishing. As indicated by its title, this text looks exclusively at the different ways to manage the physiological symptoms most often associated with terminal illnesses, leaving the spiritual and psychological aspects to others.

Heffner, John E., and Ira R. Byock. 2002. *Palliative and End-of-Life Pearls.* Philadelphia: Hanley and Belfus.

This compilation of more than 70 case studies represents contributions from prominent nurses, ethicists, religious leaders, and doctors within the palliative care community. Each patient vignette is written from the actual experiences of its author and includes a diagnosis, discussion, and summary of key points. Topics approach a wide variety of end-of-life issues, including medical treatment, spiritual care, cultural sensitivity, and communication.

Topical Issues

Communication

Heaven, Cathy, and Peter Maguire. 2003. "Communication Issues." In *Psychosocial Issues in Palliative Care,* edited by Mari Lloyd-Williams, 13–34. New York: Oxford University Press.

The authors of this selection identify factors that contribute to communication breakdown in palliative care scenarios and then briefly discuss effective ways to interview, give information, and maintain acquired communication skills.

Kuhl, David. 2002. *What Dying People Want: Practical Wisdom for the End of Life.* New York: Public Affairs.

Kuhl, a palliative care physician, tells the stories of his dying patients as well as those from literature, folktales, myths, and religious traditions. In doing so he is able to explore the spiritual and psychological aspects of dying, informing the reader, whether he is terminally ill or knows someone who is dying, about ways to navigate the process of dying. An emphasis is placed on communicating as a dying patient and communication with dying patients.

Randal, Fiona, and R. S. Downie. 1999. "Giving Information." In *Palliative Care Ethics: A Companion for All Specialists,* edited by Fiona Randal and R. S. Downie, 2d ed., 128–48. New York: Oxford University Press.

Most palliative care writings on communication explore the "how to do" aspects of communicating; this chapter, from a larger work on palliative care ethics, explores the moral obligations of a physician when giving information. It asks questions such as "How much information is the physician obligated to tell?" and "Whom is the physician obligated to tell this information to?" It also looks at the moral difficulties in giving information and revisits key points in its summary.

Longaker, Christine. 1998. *Facing Death and Finding Hope: A Guide to the Emotional and Spiritual Care of the Dying.* New York: Double Day.

Buckman, Robert. 1993. *How to Break Bad News: A Guide for Health Care Professionals.* Baltimore: Johns Hopkins University Press.

Based on the "Breaking Bad News" course at the University of Toronto, this book was intended for the use of doctors and medical students (although it is an interesting read for any health care professional). It is one of the few books that deal exclusively with how to effectively break bad news to patients. It offers case histories, sample interviews, chapter summaries, and bolded "ground rules" throughout the text.

Death and Dying

Lynn, Joanne, and Joan Harrold. 1999. *Handbook for Mortals: Guidance for People Facing Serious Illness.* New York: Oxford University Press.

This handbook is primarily written for patients with a terminal illness, although it is a worthwhile read for family members and caregivers alike. It is essentially a "roadmap" for the dying and answers questions that concern seeking help, coping with illness, seeking medical treatment, enduring bereavement, and managing pain. Information is disseminated in a reader-friendly manner, and scattered throughout the book are valuable stories, quotations, and boxes. An issue-specific and disease-specific resource list is also available at the end of the book.

Byock, Ira. 1998. *Dying Well.* New York: Riverhead Books.

A hospice director in Missoula, Montana, Byock shares 12 stories of dying patients and their families. In this collection of his personal experiences, each of which illustrates a different aspect of personal growth, he argues that death does not have to be a journey of suffering: it is possible to "die well." The book also includes a valuable question-and-answer section in the back, as well as a brief list of resources and further reading suggestions.

Nuland, Sherwin B. 1995. *How We Die: Reflections on Life's Final Chapters.* New York: Vintage Books.

This surgeon recounts his experiences with six of the most common fatal illnesses and their devastating physical and emotional effects. In his opinion, too much of the literature dealing with death and dying romanticizes the process, ultimately causing us to be unprepared for our own deaths and for the deaths of those we love. As such, his purpose in this book is to "demythologize the process of dying" and to emphasize the importance of a profound life, something we can control, over the importance of a profound deathbed scene, something we cannot.

Kubler-Ross, Elisabeth. 1969. *On Death and Dying.* New York: Macmillan.

Written by a pioneer in the field of thanatology, this work has become one of the most well-known and widely read texts on death and dying. It is not meant to be a textbook on caring for dying patients. It was in this book that Kubler-Ross introduced her "stages of grief" model.

Ethnicity and Spirituality

Stanworth, Rachel. 2004. *Recognizing Spiritual Needs in People Who Are Dying.* New York: Oxford University Press.

This book suggests ways to spiritually care for terminally ill patients and encourage their growth. It is based on the experiences of 25 hospice patients and looks at the ways in which they express their spirituality. The "language of spirit" they use is often metaphorical and independent of religion, making this suitable for a universal audience.

Wilcock, Penelope. 1997. *Spiritual Care of Dying and Bereaved People.* Harrisburg, PA: Morehouse Publishers.

The author, a hospice chaplain and Methodist minister, writes this book as encouragement for anyone who accompanies a person through the stages of dying. Although the writing is rooted in a Judeo-Christian background, this guide offers many ways to comfort and relate to dying people and can be appreciated by any reader.

Parkes, Colin Murray, Pittue Laungani, and Bill Young. 1997. *Death and Bereavement Across Cultures.* London: Routledge.

Intended for anyone working with terminally ill patients or the bereaved, this handbook looks at the traditions and beliefs of major world religions. By discussing the context in which these beliefs were formed, how they have been affected by an increasingly globalized world, and future implications, the authors hope to foster a greater sense of understanding and support.

Irish, Donald P., Kathleen F. Lindquist, and Vivian Jenkins Nelsen, eds. 1993. *Ethnic Variations in Dying, Death, and Grief.* Washington, DC: Taylor and Francis.

This volume looks at death, dying, and grief across non-dominant ethnic communities in the United States and Canada, chronicling rituals, traditions, and teachings. It looks not only at larger groups, like Mexican Americans, but also at recent immigrant groups, like the Hmong. Each section is written by a representative of that cultural tradition and includes an illustrative episode. The book is intended for any professional working in the field of death and dying.